This book is dedicated to my amazing family:
the O'Hallorans and the O'Briens

My sisters, Caroline and Jean, my brothers Gerard and Michael;
to my heartbeat, my children, Sam, Robert, Stacey and Kaya;
to my grandchildren, Aaliyah, Mason and Jaden –
Nana loves you so much; you just melt my heart

To the wonderful woman that makes my heart leap when she
holds my hand, calms my soul and soothes my heart. I am so
excited to take the next chapter in my life with you, Ismay

To my heroes, my mam and dad, Precious and Mickey O'Brien.
Your love and wisdom kept me safe in your care. I carry you
in my heart each day and feel your presence, guiding me
and loving me still

I hope I make you as proud of me as I am of you, always

INTRODUCTION

I can remember it as if it were yesterday. I'm four years of age and my friends and I are peering out of a window onto a flat roof. The roof is covered in shiny red and green apples. We've been looking at them for days, our mouths watering. We are so hungry, we can imagine biting into them, crunching down on the sweet flesh, feeling the acidic tang on our tongues.

The window is at our level and I can see myself opening it slowly, looking around to make sure there's no sign of the nuns who rule our tiny world. Then I crawl out onto the flat roof towards the bounty that's just within reach. I'm close to the edge now, stretching a hand out to grab a really delicious-looking one, when I lose my grip, tumbling through the air before landing with a soft thud.

I lie there, startled. Am I dead? I blink and look at the blue sky above me. I'm not on the hard ground of the convent, but on one of the bales of hay cut from the fields that surround it. Thank God, I think gratefully, before realising that if I'm still alive, I'm in the biggest trouble of my life.

I can't remember what the punishment was for this transgression, but my memory of it is my proof that I was there, at Mount Saint

Vincent industrial school on O'Connell Avenue, Limerick City. Of course, I've always known the truth of it, but when I was told on many occasions that there were no records of my stay here, I wondered if it was all in my head somehow. If the five years I spent in the Mount were real. I was taken away by force from my mother at two months of age and reunited with her at five-and-a-half, but sometimes I wondered if I'd made the whole thing up in my head. Maybe, I thought, I'd seen programmes in which tiny children were made to scrub the stairs until they shone, or to make sets of rosary beads until their little fingers bled. Maybe, that hadn't happened to me at all.

So I drove from my home outside the city to the convent last year. I looked at the austere grey-stone walls, the neatly-painted front door, at the tiny chapel, at the rows of white-framed windows and I wondered. There are no more apple trees and the convent is now part of the University of Limerick. But I walked around to the rear and there it was, the low window, the roof that I'd crawled out onto with my little friends, the branches of the apple trees heavy with fruit bending over our heads. How could I have thought I was imagining it all? I had not been able to trust those memories. Now, I knew that they were true. *They can't take my sight away from me*, I thought, *because this is where it happened.*

This visit reminded me that some years ago, I drove up to the Mount with my daughter, Kaya. I've always worked hard and I had a grá for cars, so I was driving a brand-new Mercedes. We turned into the drive of the convent and an elderly nun stopped us. 'Hello, can I help you? Are you visiting?' she said with a smile.

'Yes, I am,' I replied. 'I used to be here in the school.'

'Oh, you were a pupil?' she asked.

'No, unfortunately not.' I explained that I had been in the orphanage, 'Not through my choice or my mam's,' I added.

There was a short pause after which she nodded at my car. 'Well, now, didn't you do well for yourself? Look at your lovely car.'

I can still remember that when the little old nun had shuffled off into the convent, Kaya looked at me and said, 'She's got some cheek.'

'One day, she'll know who I am,' I said to her. 'Doing well for myself' wasn't about driving a Mercedes. I got rid of the car two months later, I couldn't drive it. The old nun's words just kept going around in my head. 'Didn't you do well for yourself?' But then I thought, why would I change my good heart to become bitter? I'm better than that. Doing well was about understanding who I really was, a journey that's taken me 63 years to complete.

I am no longer the tiny little girl with the big eyes and head of black curls, a lost look on her face. I did not let that place break me. I understand now that the only thing I could do to survive the Mount was to take the positive from it. I learned to be clean and tidy and neat, but also to have self-discipline and resilience.

I've met people who have come from those places and they're a shell. They're broken. I didn't want that to happen to me and thanks to my family and to so many others who helped me along the way, it didn't. When I came out of the Mount, aged five-and-a-half, my mother got back her little girl, but my new stepdad, who was always a father to me, saw a little Black child who was going to have a hard time growing up in Limerick. He needed to equip her to be strong, to withstand everything that was going to come at her at different points in her life, and he did. He gave me confidence, reassurance and love as well as passing on a passion for sport that would propel me to an international soccer and rugby career. The woman I am today is down to him and to the love and support of my mother.

In spite of these strengths and the love of my family, I never felt that I was good enough to be accepted for who I really am. Until ten years ago, I wore a heavy suit of armour to protect myself from other people and from my true self. Only recently, have I embraced Jackie O'Halloran-O'Brien-McCarthy. For all that I am: a proud, gay, Limerick, Irish, Jamaican mother, grand-mother, ex-Irish international soccer and rugby player, and a woman who lives life on my own terms.

I have written this book mostly to close that chapter in my life, to deal with my past and to put it to bed for once and for all, but also for my children to have a better understanding of their mother and the things that made me the person I am today. I want them to see the light shine through my broken parts and hopefully they can embrace all that I am. It's been a hard six months putting this down on paper, not just because of my dyslexia, but to revisit all my pain, my failures, my loss, my anger. I've often asked myself if it's worth it, but it really is. I can now understand myself at a deeper level. I can forgive my shortcom-ings, but most of all, I can embrace all of me. I can look at the photograph of me as a child with the big, sad eyes and say to her, 'We made it, kid.'

CHAPTER 1

THE MOUNT

I am a proud Limerick woman. I love every part of my city, from Thomond Park to King John's Castle, from my childhood home in Kileely to the Milk Market. But I'm not sure if my city has always loved me back, at least in the way that I wanted it to. As a Black child growing up there in the 1960s, I wanted desperately to belong, and yet I stood out. I was tall, skinny and dark-skinned, with a shock of thick black hair and was often an object of curiosity when I would walk around town.

I played on the Limerick soccer team despite people telling my mother that I would never amount to anything and that no-one would want to marry a girl like me. One of the highlights of my footballing career was playing for my country: by wearing the green jersey, no one could take my Irishness away from me. I now know that I'm gay, but when I married my husband Tom, it was out of love and because I wanted to be with someone who loved and accepted me.

Now, I understand that the twists and turns of my life were leading me to the woman I am now, who no longer feels the need to do everything possible to fit in. I am happy to be me and have found a voice that feels authentic and true to who I am. I am comfortable in my own skin. But it wasn't always that way.

My story begins with my mother, Precious Imelda O'Halloran. It's some name! It always makes me laugh because it has an almost African feel to it, but she was called after her aunt, a nun, Sister Precious Imelda. We didn't actually know her name was Precious because her sisters always called her Pat, even though her husband always referred to her as 'Presh'. Mam was one of five children, two boys and three girls. My grandmother died when my mother was very young and they were raised by my grandad Josie. An electrician by trade, he did his utmost to look after them all and to keep the family together. By the time she was a teenager, her four siblings had left for Birmingham to make new lives for themselves. Before long, my mother joined them, leaving my grandad behind. I often wonder what it must have been like to lose your whole family to emigration like that, knowing that they'd never return. What was there for them to return to? The industries that had made the city's fortune, such as lace and Limerick ham were in decline and the multinationals had yet to arrive. I know that Limerick people, including myself, don't like the depiction of our city as Stab City – we prefer the city's motto 'an ancient city fierce in the skills of war' – but it's true that there was a lot of poverty in the city at the time and a lot of unemployment.

Mam loved her new life in Birmingham, which was thriving, full of pubs and nightclubs, glamour and excitement. It felt bright and modern, completely unlike the city she'd left behind. But it was still the early 1960s, so when Mam became pregnant, she told very few people, instead slipping away to a mother and baby home for the last months of her pregnancy.

On 29 September 1961, I was born by Caesarean section in the Queen Elizabeth Hospital in Birmingham and this is where the lie about my origins began. Mam knew that I would be a child of colour, she had secretly been going out with a man of Jamaican descent, but because of the stigma that went with that, she kept the secret to herself and the lie grew from there, a lie that would colour my life until a shocking revelation in my fifties, when I discovered the truth. Whenever anyone would ask her about the pregnancy, she would say that something terrible had happened. The only person who knew the truth was Sister Precious Imelda.

Mam often told me that the song that was number one in the charts at the time was 'Take Good Care of My Baby', by Bobby Vee. Mam knew that the home would put me up for adoption, so when I was only two weeks' old, the day before a nice couple were to pay a visit with a view to adopting me, she made a run for it to her sister's, my auntie Marie.

Marie had to think on her feet, when her sister landed on her doorstep with a newborn baby. She pulled a drawer out of the chest of drawers in the bedroom and made a bed of it with a pillow inside. She held out her hands to take me from my mother, who was clinging tightly to me.

When my mother handed me to her, Marie screamed. 'Pat, where did you get the monkey from? Where in the name of God is the baby?' These words might seem shocking nowadays, but in Birmingham in 1961, a baby of colour was so unusual that my aunt didn't know how to interpret my black skin and the thick tuft of black hair standing up from my head.

My aunt didn't really have to say anything further. Mam knew that I would never be accepted and she did the only thing she

7

could: she wrote a letter to her father in Limerick, telling him the whole story. 'I'm coming home from Birmingham with my baby. She is a child of colour. If you're there to meet me, great. If you're not, I'll get back on the boat.' My grandad was my mother's only hope.

It must have been a long and anxious journey for Mam, taking the train from New Street to Holyhead, then getting on the mail-boat to Dún Laoghaire and the train to Limerick. I can see her in my mind, looking out the window at the passing fields, wondering if anyone would be there to meet her at the station. What would she have done if there was no-one there? I can imagine that she would have had to climb back up the steps of the train and make her way back to England in disgrace.

As her feet touched home again on Colbert Station's platform, she scanned the crowds anxiously for any sign of her father. He was there. He'd come to walk down the streets of Limerick city with his granddaughter in her pram, proud as punch.

With new-found confidence, my mother did the same, walking me through the streets, dressed in immaculate white dresses that her sisters had sent her from Birmingham. I was an object of curiosity and people would stop to examine me in wonder, with my lovely curls and huge brown eyes. With her father's support, Mam thrived and so did I.

On a cold November day, just two months later, there was a knock on the door that would change both of our lives forever. My mother went to open it, to find two nuns, a priest and two Gardaí standing on the doorstep. Behind them was an ambulance, its engine humming. Quietly and calmly, they asked her to hand her baby over to them. They had secured a court order to take me to an orphanage for adoption. The papers, which I still have, showed that a Father John Ryan of St Munchin's parish had applied for a section 55 order to have me removed from my home. A section 55 order under the 1953 Health Act meant that a child could be taken in to the nearest home to be looked after. This was meant to help children whose parents had died, or didn't have the means to support their family following the death of one parent, but in reality, the Catholic church used it to remove large numbers of children from their birth families.

'But she's not an orphan,' my mother protested. 'She has a family.' Her pleas fell on deaf ears. It was clear that in 1961, no unmarried woman was going to be allowed to walk the streets of Limerick with her illegitimate child, especially a child of colour. The shame and disgrace to those in charge was too much to bear. Many years later, a good friend of mam's told me that she ran after the ambulance, screaming and crying in her bare feet. But there was nothing either she or my grandad could do. The state and the church had come together to take her child away and she was powerless to resist. That was the way Ireland was then.

It still hurts me so much to think about what that day was like for Mam. Her world was rocked to its core and there was nothing she or her dad could do to fight the powers that be. She did the best that she could, but life as she knew it was over.

CHAPTER 2

THE ONLY LIFE I KNEW

My first memories of the Mount are of smells and sounds that, whenever they come back to me now, make me stop in my tracks: the cleaner that we used on the stairs that led up to the first floor, the shushing sound of the scrubbing brush as we would pass it back and forth across the stairs, me on one side, just three or four years of age, another girl on the other. If someone came down the stairs while we were cleaning them, we'd have to start all over again.

I can still smell the floor polish that we used to clean the hard floors; the sharp tang of urine in the dormitories caused by our nightly bedwetting. If we wet the bed, we would have to take our sheets and carry them to the dinner hall where we would stand by the wall, wet sheets in our hands, our breakfast bowls on our heads, while the others had their breakfast of lumpy porridge. If the bowl fell from your head, you were punished with a slap across the legs from one of the nuns. Soon, my only friend, Lilian Bond and I had worked out a scheme: we were both bed-wetters, but if we shared a bed and left the other dry, at least one of us would get a breakfast in the morning. We would take it in turns: one morning I would look on enviously as Lilian tucked in to her breakfast, the next, it would be my turn. It always surprises me how resourceful we were, even at four years of age.

I remember the loneliness that swallowed me when one day, Lilian wasn't there. There was no explanation and she was never spoken about again. I used to wonder where Lilian had gone. Maybe someone had taken her to live with them? Maybe she'd run away? I was bewildered. We weren't allowed to have friends in the Mount, but Lilian and I had formed a bond. And now she was gone. Then, one evening, we were allowed to watch a Shirley Temple film on the television. The child actress was a huge star at the time, with her head of golden curls and her sweet voice. She was singing 'Animal Crackers in My Soup'. When I saw Shirley Temple, I sat bolt upright. *There she is*, I thought. There's Lilian.

I will always remember the sound of my tummy rumbling: removing food from us was a punishment frequently doled out, so we were constantly hungry. Now, in my sixties, I only eat one meal a day. I can remember the feeling of the rosary beads as they slid through my little fingers, twisting the small piece of metal that connected one bead to the next until my fingers bled.

I can still hear the sound of the water gurgling through the huge pipes on Fridays, when we had baths. We would all be lined up, naked and shivering, waiting our turn to use the water, which would become increasingly grimy after each of us had been dunked in it and scrubbed as hard as possible. I was always last: because of my skin colour, one nun told me, I would only dirty the water for the others. Then the screams would start as the nuns fine combed our hair, pulling it as hard as possible from the roots.

Zero consideration was given to my needs as a Black child, how my hair was different to everyone else's. Our scalps would frequently bleed.

The only good thing about Friday nights was that the next day was a Saturday. Saturdays were visiting days, when family members could visit and more importantly, when the nuns would be on their best behaviour, smiling and ushering us around carefully as visitors looked on. Saturdays were also the only day in the week in which we could play freely. I used to love running around in the yard with Lilian, playing games of chase and skipping, without the nuns' beady eyes on us. I used to dread hearing my name called when I was in the middle of a game, 'Jacqueline O'Halloran'. My heart would sink because that meant that I would lose an hour of playtime to sit in a room with a stranger.

I would creep in to the visiting room to see the woman with the sad eyes sitting in a chair in front of me. When I'd come in, she would smile at me. 'Hello Jacqueline,' she would say. I would murmur a hello in reply. I had no idea who this woman was. Then the questions would begin: How was my day? Fine. How were my friends? Fine. Were the nuns kind? Yes. Was I getting enough food? Yes, I would lie. We would have been warned not to talk about anything that happened in the Mount for fear of the punishment that would follow. The woman would lean forward in her chair, words on her lips that I could sense she wanted to tell me but couldn't. All I wanted was to go back outside and play.

That woman was my mother. Every Saturday without fail, she would come and visit me in the Mount. She was told never to talk to me about who she was or why she was visiting in case she would upset me and make life harder for me. Later, I would learn that on one visit, she managed to give an older girl a half-crown and asked her to look after me as best she could. I met that girl years later and she told me I had been her charge. Little Jacqueline O'Halloran, she called me.

The Christmas visits were the worst of all. Some of us would get presents from our visitors, which we were told not to open. When my mother handed me over a box, wrapped in brightly coloured Christmas paper, I just sat there, looking at it, knowing that whatever toy was inside, I would never get to play with it. As soon as the visitors were gone, we would be lined up, our presents under our arms, and taken to another home for children or a hospital to give our presents to the child. They were less well off than ourselves, we were told. It was the Christian thing to do, after all.

I would spend five years in the Mount, the first and most formative years of my life. I learned important skills there: I learned to be neat and tidy, to be self-disciplined, to eat sparingly, to rely only on myself. Like a plant that isn't watered, I grew nonetheless, albeit in a strange and lonely direction. I was institutionalised, and the only rules I understood were the arbitrary and cruel ones of the Mount. It was the only life I knew.

CHAPTER 3

ELEPHANT GIRL

Memories can be funny things. You think you can trust them, but they have a habit of being unreliable. But I can remember the day my mother came to fetch me as if it were yesterday. It was 1966 and I was five-and-a-half years old. All I knew was the Mount. It was my prison and my home.

I'd been playing in the yard with the other children when a voice called me, 'Jacqueline O'Halloran'. If you were singled out while playing in the yard it generally meant that you had a visitor, or that you'd done something and were about to be punished. Swallowing nervously, I walked slowly towards the office, where the kind lady with the sad eyes was waiting for me. I can't remember what was said, but next thing, I was being taken by the hand, out through the gates of the Mount onto the busy streets. People bustled by carrying shopping bags and newspaper sellers yelled out the price of the *Limerick Leader*. Buses swept by and after the hush of the Mount, every noise felt painfully loud.

'It's not far,' the lady told me as I hesitated. 'Come on.' She extended a hand to me, but I didn't give her mine, even though I could see the sadness in her eyes at the rejection. But I had no idea who she was.

After a short walk through the city streets, we arrived at a warren of small modern houses that sat in the shadow of Thomond Park. The estate was part of the expansion of the city in the 1950s but was still in walking distance of King John's Castle and the River Shannon. Coming from Kileely meant that you were a true Limerick person.

When we walked in the front door of one of the houses, a man was sitting there with a small child on his lap. I didn't know him, but he smiled at me warmly. I didn't know then that this man would become such a big part of my life, my dad and my hero. The little girl was my sister, Regina. They told me this over tea, and I could see that they were friendly, but all I could think was, what time will they take me home? What had I done wrong, I wondered, to be sent here to live with people I didn't know? I wanted to go home. The Mount might have been an institution, but it was the only home I knew. It was a frightening place, full of the shouts and screams of small children, the arbitrary rules of the nuns, but it was familiar and I desperately wanted to go back.

The grown-ups asked me lots of questions about the Mount, but I didn't reply for fear I'd say something wrong. To me the questions were a trick: the man and the woman wanted to get me to say something I shouldn't about the nuns, and I would pay the price when the nuns got me back home.

After tea, the lady led me upstairs to a room with pretty wallpaper on the walls and a lovely single bed decked out in pink. It smelled so nice, not of pee, but of fresh, clean sheets. I began to panic. My worst fear, it seemed, was becoming real. I was to sleep here, on my own, without my dorm-mates. My head spun:

I can't go to sleep here, I thought. What if I wet the bed? I'll be in so much trouble. I promised God I'd be the best girl I could. I'd work really hard and not cry about my bleeding fingers when making the rosary beads if he'd just let me go home. I burst into tears and nothing the woman said could soothe me.

Eventually, I climbed into bed, worn out from the crying and exhaustion, and I lay awake, listening to the sounds of the traffic and people passing outside. Around me, the room was silent. There were no snuffles or coughs or cries from my dorm-mates. I prayed that I wouldn't wet the bed because then there would be no breakfast.

Exhausted the next morning from lack of sleep, I was delighted to see that I hadn't wet the bed. When the woman came into the bedroom and wished me good morning, I remember pulling back the bed covers to show her the bed was dry. She smiled at me and placed some clothes on the bed. 'These are for you. Can you dress yourself or do you need a hand?'

Was she crazy? Of course, I could dress myself. Hadn't I been doing it since I could stand? And now, I was over five. I nodded and she left me to get dressed, telling me to come down for breakfast then. I liked the way the woman called my name. There was no anger, no spite, just a warm-sounding 'Jacqueline'. My excitement grew. Maybe a dry bed would mean I could go home.

Downstairs, I sat at the table with the man, the woman and the little girl. The sadness I had seen in the woman's eyes was gone and she was smiling at me as she pushed a plate of sausages, bacon and pudding towards me. I had no idea what to make of it. Breakfast in the Mount was a bowl of lumpy porridge. To this day, I can't eat anything with lumps in it. I waited until I saw them beginning to eat before the lovely smell of the food got the better of me and I bit into a sausage. The taste was heaven: salty and fatty and unlike anything I'd had in the Mount.

The man began to play happily with the little girl at the table, lifting a spoon and guiding it towards her lips. As she messed around with her food, my heart almost stopped. This child is going to be punished for playing with her food, I thought, imagining one of the nuns bearing down on her, hand raised for a slap. But nothing happened. And when she tossed a bit of food onto the floor, I thought, that's done it. She's going to be in for it now. I ran to pick it up and put it back on her plate. Nothing happened apart from a 'thank you, Jacqueline,' from the man.

The rest of breakfast passed happily until the man got up and said he was off to work. He reached his hand down and ruffled the little girl's hair. 'See you, Gina,' he said. She replied with a gummy smile. He turned to me then, and seeing the fear in my eyes, he just smiled gently and said goodbye.

This was most people's experience of breakfast but to me, it was totally alien. Where was the crashing and banging of trays, bowls and cutlery? Where were the slaps to the back of the head for not eating properly? This seemed too good to be true. I managed to sneak some food into my pocket, so that when I got home to the Mount, I could show the other children the strange food these people ate.

The woman then stood and started to clean away the breakfast dishes. I jumped up to help, as usual, but the woman just said, 'No, just play with your sister. I'll do the washing-up.' *What is she talking about?* I wondered. This child isn't my sister. I sat there uneasily until the woman called me upstairs. She dressed the little girl so gently and in such a playful way, it amazed me. I'd never been played with like that in the Mount. We had been dressed in our little smocks by impatient, rough hands, ready to belt us if we didn't get on with it quickly.

Once Regina was dressed, the lady carried her downstairs and put her gently in her pram. She turned to a lovely red coat hanging on a coat hook in the hall. 'This is for you, Jacqueline.' She got it down and tried to put it on me. I backed away. She just smiled and said, 'Sorry, I forgot you're a big girl and you can do it yourself.' She smiled when she said this, but the sadness was back in her eyes. I couldn't help thinking, *good, maybe that means I'm going home.*

As we opened the front door the first thing that hit me was the sound of children laughing as they played a game on the street. I wasn't used to loud playing, to jumping and yelling with excitement, as we had always been told that good little girls and boys played quietly. As the woman pushed the pram along the street, I walked, not by her side, but a little bit behind her. She reached out her hand to me, but I just put my head down. Once again, the sadness was back in her eyes.

As we walked along, a group of children began to gather around us, staring and pointing, as if something extraordinary had appeared in front of them. Then I realised it was me. I was the one they were marvelling at, probably the first child of colour they had ever seen. I didn't understand their curiosity, the pushing and jostling to get closer to me and I shrunk back into myself. Next, it was the grown-ups: they all knew the lady and they stopped to see this strange child walking about Kileely. There were 'ohs' and 'aahs' and, 'God bless her, isn't she like a doll?'

One woman exclaimed, 'Look at her big brown eyes and her hair – doesn't she look exotic?' In spite of the remarks, the women all smiled at me, warm expressions in their eyes. I didn't know then that a lot of those women were friends of my mam and would take me to their hearts. In response, the woman smiled at me, a look of pride in her eyes. She was clearly a nice lady, I thought, but as she showed me around the place – the handball alley which would become my playground, the school I would attend – I began to suspect that something was wrong. I wasn't going back 'home' to the Mount. This strange, busy place was to become my home.

That night the friendly man came home from work along with a crowd of grown-ups, who he introduced as his brothers and sisters. Again, the comments started: 'Isn't she lovely? What does she sound like when she talks?' I could see the nice lady becoming angry with their questions and instinctively, I knew how she felt. Later that evening, when I was shown the lovely smelling room again, I put on my night dress by myself and knelt down by the side of the bed to say my prayers. 'Dear God, please let me go home again. I'll do my best to be good if you can make this happen. Amen.'

When the woman came in to say goodnight, she sat down on the bed and reached out to push my hair back from my face, but I pulled away. With her sad eyes she said, 'Jacqueline, this is your home. You're not going back to that horrible place.'

I closed my eyes thinking, *what did I do wrong? This is not my home.* But no-one explained the situation to me, as far as I can remember. No-one told me why my new family was White while I was Black. *Maybe*, I thought, *my real family is out there somewhere, looking for me.* In the meantime, I couldn't settle with these people. I felt that I didn't belong.

For the next two years, I ran away almost every day, making it as far as the bus stop before deciding that I was too hungry to make it any further. One evening when I was about seven, I settled on the sofa after tea to watch the TV and came across a programme called *Elephant Boy*. The little boy in the show was an orphan and he was Indian. As I looked at him sitting on top of an elephant, travelling all over the country in search of his parents, something clicked. The people I lived with didn't look like me, but the boy did with his dark skin and hair. Maybe my parents were in India or Africa looking for me. The more I thought about it, the more it made sense. I was just being minded here until my real family came for me. I was Elephant Girl.

In 1967, a year after I left the Mount, my sister Caroline was born. She had a head of golden hair and looked so much like mam, who was small with a lovely smile and vivid green eyes that leaped from her face. I had no interest in this crying, noisy baby that seemed to give her parents so much joy, but I appreciated the good food, the nice clothes and the clean bed that I continued to wet. I was never punished for wetting the bed, which took me a while to get my head around. Instead, the woman who was my mother would calmly strip the bed and pop the sheets into the wash, the clothes-line always full of bed sheets, flapping in the wind and rain.

One day in 1968, the woman disappeared for a few days and when she came back, she placed the cutest little bundle in my arms, saying, 'This is your baby brother, Gerard.' I didn't understand the warm feeling that spread through me as I looked at him, but I instinctively wanted to look after him. Just as the older girls in the Mount would look after the babies, I looked after Gerard. I insisted that his cot be put in my room, so I could make sure he was safe. With the baby in the room beside me, gurgling away, I felt a newfound sense of safety, a sense that the man, the woman and the two little girls would become Mam, Dad, my sisters and then my brother. I was going to fit in. I wanted to belong.

CHAPTER 4

HALF OF EVERYTHING

My mother's little baby girl had been taken away from her and what she'd got back was a tough little tomboy, who didn't want to wear pink dresses or play with dolls or prams. Years later, all of this would make more sense, but as a child, I could not express what I could barely feel. I was a part of this family unit and yet at the same time, I wasn't. I belonged and at the same time, many people around me thought that I didn't. The woman's big smile when I called her Mam gave me a warm feeling. I felt protective of my sisters and brother, but because we looked so different, people thought that we couldn't possibly be related.

My mother would try to put me in the lovely dresses her sisters sent her from England, but I was having none of it. All I wanted to do was to wear trousers or shorts and kick a football with the boys. I loved games of Cowboys and Indians and clambering over the walls of the local big house to steal apples – 'skinning orchards' was one of our favourite things to do. The girls I found hard to understand. They seemed to be much more complicated, standoffish, huddled into little groups around a doll or a pram. I knew that Mam was disappointed but Dad would just say, 'Leave her alone, Presh. Let her go out and play. Let her kick a football. What does it matter what she wears?' A champion handball player himself, he recognised my eye for a ball and my quickness on my feet and he always encouraged it. This is where my bond with Dad began.

Mam realised she was fighting a losing battle. I was never going to change. I was never going to be her pretty little girl in pink. She'd lost her baby in her gorgeous white frilled dresses, and she'd got back a child who hated dresses and frills and anything girly. She'd left behind a soft little baby with big eyes and chubby cheeks and she'd got back a hard, skinny little girl, who was frightened and who had no idea what love looked like. I was slow to bond with Mam because I wasn't the child she'd imagined in her head for five long years. She wasn't the mother I'd imagined either – because when I closed my eyes at night, hearing the snuffling of all of the other little bodies around me, I hadn't imagined anyone at all.

Our fragile relationship wasn't helped when, six months into her pregnancy with her fifth child, she became unwell and was rushed to the hospital. Later, I would learn that she knew something was horribly wrong, even though the staff assured her that all was well. Left in a room on her own, she gave birth to a baby who was stillborn. On top of this she had been given a pint of blood from the incorrect blood group, which flooded her pituitary glands. She lost all of her hair and became extremely unwell.

It was a time of confusion and mystery to those of us at home. Even though my aunt Joan returned from Birmingham to look after us, as well as Dad's brothers and sisters pitching in, we really had no idea what was going on. In those days, nothing was ever discussed or shared with children. All I knew was that my bond with Mam was broken before it had really ever been repaired.

When she returned from hospital, I resented her for having left me again. I didn't understand the stupid wig she was wearing or why she spent so much time in bed. As a resentful little girl, I thought she was just being lazy. I didn't like having to help more around the house and look after my siblings, because it ate into my precious play time, running around on the streets with a ball. Mam and I would have many running battles at this time and I could feel the resentment, see it in her eyes. I had bonded with Dad in a way that I hadn't with her and I had grown closer to my O'Brien cousins. In fact, I was proud to call myself Jackie O'Brien now. I didn't know that Dad hadn't adopted me: that he'd been told not to waste his good name on me.

I would learn later that she was unable to have any more children, which must have been devastating to her, but as a child, I could only see things from my own perspective. To me, Mam was weary and low in mood, ready to snap at the slightest thing. It made me even more wary of her.

It was also a hard time for us as a family. I knew that we had very little money because of the cuts of meat we would eat: breast-bones and eye-bones, pig's tails, skirts, kidneys, tripe – these were our staples, because they were cheap. They were tastier than what I'd got in the Mount, but when I'd go to the butcher's with Mam, I would eye the huge steaks or the legs of lamb and my mouth would water. Dad was on the dole, too, unable to find steady work. Instead, he worked 'tommers' as we called it, nixers, one-off jobs that paid in cash.

Like so many families, we got food on 'tick' at the local shop, the shopkeeper making a careful note of purchases in a big ledger, which would be paid off on dole day or when the children's allowance would be paid. Once a month Mam would send me to the shop with a note to get her a packet of Quality Street. I would then pocket the note when the shopkeeper wasn't looking and a few days later, I would go and use the note again to get a packet of Quality Street for myself. How I looked forward to opening the bag and unwrapping the bright purple foil of the hazelnut and caramel chocolate, the orange wrapper of the toffee, gulping them all down before I got home.

I thought I was being very clever, but when Mam asked the shopkeeper why the grocery bill was so high when she came to pay it off, she got a nasty shock. 'Well,' he said, 'if you didn't indulge in so many packets of sweets, it wouldn't be so high.' My mother could have killed me. By that stage, I'd got months out of the ruse, but it certainly didn't help my relationship with Mam, which became even more brittle.

With not a lot of work coming in, Dad fell into the habit of spending time with his brothers Christy and Paddy in the hand-ball alley, then in the pub. Sometimes, when there was no work, he could go for weeks just drinking every day. The fights kicked off between him and Mam when he returned after a session. Mam complained about the lack of money to pay the bills or to buy food. Dad always promised to stop drinking and get work, and he always tried, but weeks or months later, he fell back to his old habits.

Mam could never understand why, even with my dad's drinking, my bond was so much stronger with him when I was a child.

The truth was, he was my hero. He stood up for me against everyone. Many a salesman who called to the door found himself turfed out into the front garden for saying, 'Look at the little Black child.' And, as a tomboy, I followed him everywhere. He taught me to play handball and football and I'd go hunting with him and his brothers, learning to skin rabbits and to fish. I'd even go with him to the odd nixer, where he'd show me how to do jobs, like changing a plug and a light fitting. He never once said, 'Girls can't do this.' I learned so much from him.

But it was hard to ignore the fact that he was still a problem drinker. The fact that, at the time, work was hard to find and many men lived in the pub didn't help, as it was all too easy for Dad to head there and stay there every evening, leaving Mam at home to mind us and to worry about where the next meal was coming from. Finally, after many bouts of binge drinking, Dad announced he was going to open a grocery shop. He turned what was my bedroom into a small shop, which I wasn't happy about. It was ironic that the bedroom I'd been so afraid of when I first arrived became my refuge from the world after a while. Now, the four of us had to share one big bedroom with two double beds: my two sisters shared one and me and Gerard, my shadow, slept in the other.

Mam must have found it hurtful that I looked up to Dad so much when he left her picking up the pieces over and over again. I didn't give her credit for her sheer strength, keeping the family together and the wolf from the door. Often, after one too many, Dad would be unable to work and Mam had to run the shop while I looked after my brother and sisters. I was just ten at the time.

St Munchin's school became my escape. I loved it but I found it hard to understand. I knew that there was something different about the way I learned, but I instinctively knew how to hide it from my teachers. Because I'd learned a lot at the Mount, I was actually ahead of many of my classmates in primary school and was easily bored. My copybooks were a mess of crossings-out and poor spelling, but it was only much later that I'd be diagnosed with dyslexia. My dad also loved reading and writing, even though he, too, had left school early.

I was also struggling with being an outsider. Once, when I was about 11 in class, a nun called me 'Blackie O'Brien'. She drew a circle on the blackboard and put white dots in the middle of the circle. Then she started to cover the white dots with the purple chalk. 'Now,' she said, 'the purple dots represent Black men like Jacqueline's father, who came to Ireland in banana boats to impregnate our women.' She put down the chalk with a clunk and looked at me expectantly. I had no idea what she was talking about, even though loathing and anger radiated from her. Nobody said a word.

I didn't want to cause trouble, so I said nothing at home about the incident, but my cousins, who were in the same class as me, told my father. It took all Mam's powers of persuasion to stop him from marching into school and dealing with the situation. I overheard her talking to her sisters on the phone one evening: 'If Mickey goes into the school, he'll end up in jail because he'll probably kill that nun for the things she said about Jackie.' I took her literally and spent the next few weeks terrified that my dad would go to jail if he came near the school. In the end, I changed class and nothing further was said.

My next teacher, Rita Spring, changed my life. She gave me a love of poetry and words, in spite of my difficulties, and she became my mentor and support in school. She always reminded me of my worth as a human being and without her, I would have been lost. Everyone should have a Rita Spring in their lives. I was devastated when she died in 2016. I still use her Mass card as my bookmark.

I had a few girl friends who lived in Kileely and I thought we were on good terms, but on one occasion, I happened to sneak up on them when they were smoking in the bicycle shed. As I stood outside ready to frighten the life out of them pretending to be one of the teachers, I overheard the conversation. One of the girls said, 'How is she Black and living with a White family?'

'I don't know,' another girl answered.

'I wonder where her real parents are? She couldn't be one of the O'Briens looking like that.'

This wasn't something I wanted Dad to deal with. I was a quiet child and shy, but even so, I felt so angry and hurt that I kicked in the door of the shed and started to hit out at the girls inside. It was as if rage possessed me. The next thing, I felt a hand on my shoulder and I turned to see Miss Spring standing quietly beside me. 'Girls, off you go back to class,' she said firmly. 'Jacqueline, follow me.'

I thought that I was in huge trouble and that the school would probably call my parents. Instead, Miss Spring took me to the staff room, which was empty. She sat me down on a chair and gave me a tissue to dry my eyes and a moment to calm down. 'What happened?' she asked.

I told her about the girls talking about my family and how much it had hurt. 'But then my real family are probably in Africa looking for me as I must have been taken from them as a baby,' I added, telling her all about the Indian boy on the elephant looking for his family. I must have sounded so naïve. I could see the sadness in her eyes as she explained to me that what I had thought to be the truth just wasn't. 'The woman you call Mam is your real Mam, Jackie' she explained. 'The man you call Dad is your Mam's husband, but not your real father. Your sisters and brother are your half-sisters and brother,' she said gently.

The biggest part of what she told me was that I was only half-Black. My real father was probably in Birmingham with a family too. *He didn't want me*, I thought miserably. My world was upside down again. I felt I didn't belong. Everything was in halves: half-Black, half-sister, half-brother. And Dad was their father, not mine. My mother was the only person I could fully call my own. Why hadn't they told me? Why had they left me imagining that they'd adopted me to keep me safe for my real family? My proud name, O'Brien, wasn't even mine.

It took me a long time to get over the shock of this day. Now, I could understand why the colour of my skin was a problem for people. Now, I knew why all the American tourists stopped to take pictures and give me money when I made my First Communion. They hadn't seen or expected to see a little Black child in a white dress in White Ireland. *I was all alone*, I thought. There was no-one in Limerick like me.

Then something happened to change that. After a trip to the doctor with a bad cough, Dad, a 60-a-day smoker, was told he had TB and was sent to Merlin Park, Galway for treatment, which lasted over three months. I had just started secondary school and was excited to be mixing with people from other parts of the city, but while Dad was in hospital, I had to leave school to help Mam in the shop. As I couldn't drive, I would push a big pram to the cash-and-carry to pick up supplies for the shop. I would lift up to forty bales of briquettes and forty bags of potatoes onto the shelves. It was good to be needed, even though I longed to be in school with my friends.

One day, I was in the shop when there was a tournament going on in the handball alley. A group of 13- and 14-year-old boys from Weston, in the south of the city, came into the shop for lemonade while I was scrambling around underneath the counter for stock. When I popped my head back up, I was greeted by two Black faces. I screamed.

Hearing my screams, Mam came running out and hastily served the two boys, as we looked at each other in amazement. I couldn't move or open my mouth. All I could think was, *oh my God, there are more of us. I'm not alone after all.*

Later on, Mam explained that as far as she knew there were four of us children of colour living in Limerick. They all had White mothers and Black fathers, none of whom were to be seen. I spent that night just looking at my hands and my face in the mirror, really seeing my colour for the first time.

CHAPTER 5

KEEP YOUR EYES LEVEL

I never went back to school. Dad's recovery from TB was slow and if I'd returned to school, I'd have to struggle with my learning again. But what was really important to me at the time was that all my friends would have moved on without me. I didn't want to be the odd one out again. So I left and worked in the shop, just like the dad I idolised.

As a child, I spent a lot of time in my own head, daydreaming. Being shy and awkward, I didn't have very many friends, so living in a world of my imagination was a comfort to me. When things were too hard, I could disappear into my thoughts as I ran laps of the local park. I was a good runner, fast, with lots of stamina and very quickly, running became my way of staying sane. It was also my way of getting away: in my head, I was running back to the Mount, where things were at least predictable, or back to my family in Africa. I had this idea that if I became famous in sport, my family in Africa might see me on TV and come to get me and bring me home.

I joined a local running club and after about six months, I started to go to the park when the coach or the club wasn't there. I wanted to be a better runner than the rest, so I would train harder than everyone. As I ran, my dad's words would ring in my ears. 'If you want something in life, you have to work hard for it.' I knew that he was right, and so I kept going around and around, testing myself on my speed, enjoying the feeling of being strong and going faster. It came naturally to me. I found so many things difficult, like friendship and school and my place in the family but running? That I could do.

One day, I arrived at the park and I noticed a group of girls and boys kicking a football around the pitch. I suppressed the flicker of annoyance at this group invading my space and got started. On my third or fourth lap a ball flew across my path and, without thinking, I met it with my right foot and kicked it back towards the group, continuing my run. As I was coming out of a bend, I noticed a man in front of me, waiting. I got closer and he stepped in my path and held up his hand. *Oh no,* I thought, *here we go: he's going to give out to me about the stupid ball.* I drew to a halt, bending over to catch my breath. 'Hi,' he said softly. 'My name is Junior Keane. Can I talk to you for a minute?'

I stood there warily as he told me that I had a 'sweet right foot', which I didn't understand. I was only 11 after all, and the other girls on the pitch looked a lot older than me. 'I'm starting a woman's football team,' he said then, calling the girls over to meet me and they introduced themselves one by one. 'Come on and join in,' said a tall girl called Marion, pulling me gently by the shoulders onto the pitch. She passed the ball to me and I passed it back. It was so easy. I remember thinking, this is great: no-one is asking me questions about my family or my colour. They just want to kick a bloody ball.

My head went up as my confidence grew and I realised that I was really good at this. The ball seemed to connect to my foot with ease and I could pass and kick with accuracy and speed. *I can't wait to tell Dad*, I thought. He was a great soccer player and now, I could be just like him. Within a minute, I lost concentration and a rocket of a shot hit me full on the chest, knocking the wind from my whole body. I fell to the ground so embarrassed and waited for the girls to start laughing at me as I lay on the ground, winded, fighting the tears that were building in my eyes. There was no laughter though, as the girls gathered around me. 'You'll be okay in a minute,' said one of them. 'Just take a breath.' She patted me gently on the head. I'd never been treated this way before, with understanding and patience. I sat there with my sore chest, astonished.

When the game came to an end, Junior offered me a lift home, first asking me who my parents were and where I lived. 'Mickey and Precious O'Brien from Kileely,' I told him.

'I know your dad well,' he said, ushering me into the car and driving me the short distance home. I was secretly pleased to get a lift because my chest was still sore, but I also knew that Mam would kill me for getting into a car with a stranger. I could see her face, 'How many times do I have to tell you, Jackie?' Sure enough, when my parents saw the car pull up in front of the house, they both came rushing out. 'What happened to her?' my dad asked Junior.

'It's okay,' Junior said. 'She was just kicking the ball around with my women's team and she winded herself. She's very good, you know. I'd really like her to join the team.'

I will never forget the smile on Dad's face. It was a look I would come to know as one of pride. Frank 'Junior' Keane had asked his daughter to join the very first Limerick Ladies' soccer team.

'All she needs is a good pair of boots,' Junior added. My mother gave him a look, because we didn't have that kind of money.

'I don't care, Mam,' I said. 'I'll play in my tackies if I have to.' Tackies was the Limerick word for trainers. The word actually came from South African employees of De Beers Diamonds in Shannon and had somehow overtaken the local term of 'runners'. Frankly, I didn't care if I had to play in my bare feet. I wanted to get that feeling back that I'd had on the pitch: the freedom of it, the joy of belonging.

With my parents' reluctant permission, I joined Limerick Ladies and began to live for the training sessions with my teammates. I was only 11 – a tall 11, yes, but a young girl – and the other girls were much older. Some of them even had jobs or boyfriends, but they really looked after me. It was a whole new world for me and I loved it.

But after a few weeks my tackies were wrecked. I had no idea how I was going to play now, and one Tuesday evening as I got to the gates of the park, one of the girls was waiting for me, a shoe box in her hand and a big smile on her face. She handed it to me and said, 'These are for you. Now, hurry up we're waiting for you to start training,' and she ran off to join the others on the pitch.

I opened the box and looked at a brand new pair of soccer boots. I couldn't believe someone could be so kind to me. I later learned that the girls had all chipped in to buy them for me. It was the nicest thing that anyone had ever done for me. When I got onto the pitch in my brand-new boots, one of the girls said,

'You've no excuse not to score now.' I didn't know how to thank them but I remember that I scored all around me. *These boots are magic*, I thought.

I sprinted home that night to show off my new treasured possession to my parents and soon, my soccer training began to pay off. By the following year, 1973, when I was just 12, I was flying. The women's League of Ireland was created and Limerick Ladies was the first to win it. Imagine, me, playing on the LFAI cup-winning team! A year or so later, I would be playing for my county. I got my picture in the paper and a few write-ups from impressed pundits, about how good I could become as a player and how talented I was. My head was up and I'd walk the streets of Limerick with pride. Complete strangers would come up and pat me on the back, congratulating me on the win. These were the same people who had once told my mother that I'd never amount to anything. That no-one would marry a girl of colour like me and that the best I could hope for was a cleaning job or, as one person said, 'becoming the local bike'. Instead, here I was, part of a great team that treated me as an equal. For the first time in my life, I felt that I truly belonged. What's more, we were history-makers. In 2023, we gathered at a civic reception in Limerick to commemorate the golden jubilee of our historic win and it felt wonderful to meet all of my old teammates and to relive the memories of our wins. Four of us would go on to play for Ireland.

In 1974, a few months into my second season with the team, we were to travel to Drogheda for a match. I was so excited, I could hardly sleep the night before. Mam and Dad were up at the crack of dawn to make sandwiches and to help me to get ready for the journey. Dad polished my boots and stuffed them with newspaper and even Mam, who always looked as if she were worried about me, had a proud look in her eyes. I can still remember sitting on the stairs, the front door open. I was playing the game in my head while waiting for the minibus to pull up outside my house.

The agreed time of eight o'clock came and went with no sign of the bus. 'It's fine, pet,' Mam said to me. 'The bus is just running late.'

At half-past nine I was still sitting on the stairs, my tears starting to fall. I knew the bus wasn't coming for me. I was resigned to it, but the anger I saw in my dad's face was like nothing I'd ever seen before. 'Close the front door, Presh,' he said, a look of cold fury in his eyes. I wouldn't be going to Drogheda now.

That night, I cried myself to sleep. I couldn't understand why they hadn't come to collect me. I was a member of the team, after all. Didn't I matter to them? I'd thought that we were all friends and that I was essential to the team's success. *Maybe I was wrong*, I thought miserably.

The next morning, still upset and with no sleep and a wet pillow from my tears, Dad knocked on my bedroom door. 'Up you get, Jackie. We're going out.' I knew instantly where we were going. As we walked down the front path, I had to almost run to keep up with Dad's stride. I could feel the anger in each of his steps as we crossed the road and walked up the hill to Ballynanty, where Junior Keane lived. When Junior caught sight of Dad from behind the counter of his shop, he immediately put his hands up, as if surrendering. 'Look, the guy I hired to drive the bus forgot to pick Jackie up,' he explained, 'and the girls thought she wasn't coming because of her age. It'll never happen again.'

With a face like thunder, Dad retorted, 'Too right it will never happen again, because my daughter will never play for your team again.'

I couldn't believe my ears as my tears once again started to flow. I didn't want this to happen. I wanted to keep playing with the girls on the team. Dad placed his hands firmly on my shoulders and turned me and walked me out of Junior's shop. As I left, I caught a glimpse of Junior, mouth open in shock.

On the walk home I pleaded with Dad to allow me to play, telling him that it wasn't Junior's fault but whoever the stupid bus driver was. Dad stopped dead in the street and bent over until his eyes were level with mine. 'Jacqueline, if they don't think enough of you to pick you up, then you don't need them. You're not above anyone but you're also not below anyone. Junior put you below the rest of the girls and no-one does that to my daughter.' Then he said something I've never forgotten. 'Keep your eyes level.' What he meant by this was that I was equal to everyone – not better, not worse, but deserving of equal respect. And I hadn't got it. I was heartbroken at the time. The world as I knew it had fallen apart. I felt hurt and embarrassed that Dad had behaved like this and worse, ruined my chances with the team.

'C'mon,' he said gently. 'We'll find you another team to play with.' Sure enough, it wasn't long before St Mary's Park soccer team came calling. While I was happy to be back playing, I missed my old teammates and had to get over my shyness once again to fit in. Then Dad started to come to watch my matches and give me a few tips. Now, I think he was looking for forgiveness.

After the visit to Junior, I didn't really talk much to Dad. I turned down his invitations to go rabbit hunting or fishing, two things I would normally have leapt at the chance to do with him, tomboy that I was. As an adult, I can see that he was only defending me and encouraging me never to accept being less than others. It's a lesson I've taken with me into adulthood. But back then, I found it hard to forgive him. He'd taken away my happiness, I thought, and my confidence. However, as I began to score a lot of goals with St Mary's Park, and I listened to his advice, I realised that it was time to forgive him. 'Can I go hunting with you the next time you're going?' I asked one day. A beam spread across his face. 'Of course. We'll go tomorrow.' My relationship with Dad was back on track.

In spite of the success of Mam and Dad's shop, Dad was still drinking. Things might have looked good on the outside, with a new car sitting in front of the house and a brand new TV inside, but Dad's binges were getting worse. Once, when I was about fifteen, after a weekend playing soccer for one of the local teams, he headed to the pub with the other men. But while others on the team could drink a pint or two and go home, Dad would start drinking and not be able to stop. Mam worried desperately and we all wondered how long this binge would last. In the end, it went on for weeks until, one Sunday night, Dad came home from the pub with a friend and started to look for his car keys to drive the man home. Dad was swaying on his feet and in no condition to drive and Mam pleaded with him not to. To our surprise, he agreed. 'Fine,' he said. Then he turned to me and tossed the keys in my direction. 'You drive.'

I clutched the keys in my hand, terrified. I had had the sum total of two driving lessons at this point, both in the industrial estate around the corner. Seeing my hesitation, Dad said, 'Okay, I'll do it then,' and reached out for the keys.

'No, no, I'll do it,' I protested. 'I'll drive him home.' I can still remember the look of terror in Mam's eyes. 'It's okay,' I reassured her. 'I can do this. Dad will be in the passenger seat,' I added, looking at Dad doubtfully. We all clambered into the car, Dad wobbling into the seat beside me. 'Take your time,' he said, 'and it'll all be okay.' I took him at his word as I bunny hopped around the corner until eventually, I got going. Thankfully, the man lived not too far away, in Saint Mary's Park, even if I had to chug over the Shannon to King's Island. I thanked God it was a quiet time of night. I managed to get Dad's friend home and conking out only two more times, I got Dad back home safely. I could feel the sweat rolling down my back.

As I pulled up to the kerb with a final judder, Mam was waiting at the door. I could see the relief on her face, but I knew what lay ahead. I headed up the stairs to make sure that my brother and sisters were asleep, then slipped into bed. I lay there, listening to the argument go on until the early hours of the morning. I could hear Mam asking Dad how on earth he could let a fifteen-year-old drive across the Shannon like that, Dad's reply muffled. Eventually, I heard Mam's footsteps on the stairs and her bedroom door closed softly. From the crashing around downstairs, I understood that Dad was in the living room and would probably sleep on the sofa.

The next morning, I came down to the kitchen and was surprised to see Dad up and in great form. 'I'm sorry for making you drive,' he said. 'I'll make sure to get you some lessons.' Then he told me to gather any cigarettes I could find around the house, which I did. When Mam came down the stairs, he greeted her with a 'Good morning, Presh.'

'Good morning,' my mother replied, looking at him warily.

'I have an announcement to make, he said. 'I swear on my children's lives that I'll give up the cigarettes and I'll never drink again.' There was a long silence while we took in this information before Mam went to put on the kettle. It was clear that she didn't believe him, but true to his word, he just stopped. Dad would never drink or smoke again.

That was Dad all over: once he got the bit between his teeth, there was no stopping him. Sometimes, the outcome of that was positive, sometimes less so, but he was always firm in his resolve. I never doubted his love for me, whereas Mam and I had a more difficult relationship. Later, I would understand just how much our bond had been broken by those five years at the Mount, but as a teenager, eager for the reassurance and the safety that I felt I wasn't getting from Mam, Dad was my hero and my guiding light.

CHAPTER 6

A CHIP ON BOTH SHOULDERS

I have always loved music and when I was 15, I found it easier to pick a song to express how I was feeling rather than expressing myself in words. Lyrics were so important to me and I often learned them off by heart. I used to think that my love of music came from Mam, because she would sing as she would work in the kitchen making dinner and sometimes, she'd dance with my sisters Regina and Caroline. They would beckon me to join in, but I was so shy and self-conscious, I'd always refuse. I felt awkward in my long skinny body. I felt I had no rhythm. Later, I would learn that my mother wasn't the only music-lover in my family, and that my love of music might have come from elsewhere, but as a teenager, I had no idea that that might be the case.

With my new teammates at St Mary's Park, I started to venture into town more. Once or twice a week, I would go to a pool hall called Chalk and Cue. I liked it in there because the music playing on the jukebox was great and I could pretend that I was a real grown-up, playing pool with my friends and hanging around. But going to town was a mixed blessing: with so few other Black people in the city, the stares and the pointing would begin.

What was worse for me was at this time, 1977, Alex Hailey's drama *Roots*, about the history of an African-American family, was on television and everybody watched it, so I'd hear shouts of, 'Here, Kizzy,' or 'Look, it's Chicken George,' from passers-by. They'd taken the drama literally and clearly assumed that I was one of 'them', descended from slaves.

To try and hold my head up, I took on the persona of a hard nut, walking around with my shoulders back and head high. If someone looked in my direction, I would give them a long cold stare until they looked away. When I played soccer, my colour didn't matter, but now, I was that person again: the odd one out. At the same time, I would watch the show on the TV every Sunday and get a sense that these people were like me in some way. I wondered if their history was my history. Often, I wanted to ask Mam, but I didn't dare. I knew that the subject wasn't up for discussion. I sometimes joke that I was now so well balanced that I had a chip on both shoulders, but even if I presented a hard shell to the outside world, inside I was a mass of nerves. I was to carry this sense of there being two Jackies for a very long time.

One afternoon, when I was 16, with extra pocket money in my hand, I jogged into the pool hall, hoping to meet some of my soccer teammates. As I walked in, I scanned the crowds to see if there was any sign of them, but instead, I saw four girls in school uniform gathered around a pool table. They stopped their game and looked at me. I did my usual and gave them the cold stare and they went back to their game. I was left standing there, unsure what to do. I knew that, if I walked out, I would never go back there again and I loved the place.

God only knows where I got the guts to do what I did next. I walked to the jukebox, selected three of my favourite songs, pressed 'play' and then I walked to the pool table and slammed my money down. 'I'll play the winner,' I announced confidently. Three of the girls didn't look at me, or were afraid to do so, but the fourth potted the black ball, looked up at me and said, 'Right, so, you're playing me.'

My legs were shaking as I put my money in the slot and set up the balls. The three other girls stood back, heads down any time I looked in their direction, but this other girl was different. She stood with an air of confidence about her and had the most beautiful smile. She unnerved me a bit as she was just as good a player as me. What would I do if she beat me? I'd have to do the long walk to the door with my tail between my legs.

I played as if my life depended on it. To lose face in front of these girls would kill me. My pride was at stake here. The game was neck and neck the whole way through. When she missed with only the black ball to pot, I couldn't believe it. I stepped up to the table, shaking like a leaf. The red and black remained on the table, two easy pots. I steadied myself, potted the red and as I set myself up on the black ball, I prayed to God and all that was holy to please let me pot the black. The ball seemed to take forever to roll towards the top right-hand pocket, before slowly dropping in. I had won. It was as if I'd won the world cup. I wanted to jump up and down. I wanted to hug this girl, but instead I just stood there, not knowing what to do next, completely tongue-tied.

The girl spoke then. 'Good game. Do you want to go again?' She looked at the other three who shook their heads to say that they didn't want to play me. 'Right, so,' she said. 'This time I'm going to beat your ass.'

We began to play. Between shots, the girl asked me lots of questions about where I was from and what school I went to. I was a bit embarrassed to admit that I wasn't in school, but by this stage, Dad had given me my own premises – a repurposed garden shed – and some stock to sell vegetables and fresh chicken at the weekends after Mass. I plucked the chickens myself! And even though she was from the posh part of town, the girl seemed to be impressed that I had my own business. The other three girls joined in the conversation and to my surprise, I started to relax and ask questions in return. I didn't even care that the girl had wiped me out on the pool table.

After the game, we sat around the jukebox talking and listening to Kate Bush. I remember thinking that the girl looked just like her. Everything about this girl was beautiful: her hair, her smile, her laughter, the way she talked. Even though they were all posh and went to a posh school, they were still happy to chat to me, with my bogger accent and three-year-old tracksuit. They even laughed at my jokes. I'd never really connected with other people in this way, simply by chatting to them. On my soccer teams, we had an instant connection through play, but off the field, I was painfully shy. However, I'd discovered that humour was a great way of getting people to like me and feel at ease with me, and these four girls seemed to like my barrage of jokes. I didn't want the day to end, so when they were leaving, I told them that I came to Chalk and Cue most days.

We all said goodbye and promised to see one another again. Running home, I was on a high. This had been the best day of my life, I thought. They seemed to like me for me. There had been no mention of my skin colour or my family or where I belonged. I was elated and I couldn't wait to meet my new friends again. True to their word, they appeared the following week in the pool hall and a strong friendship grew. I spent time with them in their part of the city, with its leafy streets and fine detached houses, but if they asked to come to mine, I would always make an excuse. I was a bit embarrassed that I came from humble Kileely and my dad owned a little shop attached to the house. However, I was proud to invite them to watch me playing football and I always seemed to play so much better with them on the sideline. Maybe I showed off a bit to impress them, but I felt protected in their company: if anyone on the other team or in those watching would tell racist jokes or roar the 'N' word across the pitch, the girls would tell them to fuck off. I was delighted to have my very own squad of girls who would always look out for me. I had never experienced that before.

Soon, we started to go Sunday-afternoon discos in St John's Pavilion, a city-centre dancehall that had once hosted the likes of Thin Lizzy. We would buy lemonade and bars of chocolate and act like grownups, even though we were only 15 and 16. The girls would be asked up dancing by boys, but I never was. I didn't care: I loved listening to the music and watching my friends dance, especially Kate, or my Kate Bush, as I called her. All the boys would want to dance with her but she didn't seem interested in them. This made me happy for some strange reason.

At this stage, after years of being tall and thin, my body had started to change and I didn't like it one bit. I hated my new boobs because they didn't go with my tomboy image of myself.

I didn't think that I was a boy but I didn't want to be a girl either. I had no idea what to wear, so I asked if Kate would come with me to buy an outfit for that year's St Patrick's Day. I put myself in her hands and we browsed the rails in the shops until she found an outfit she liked. To my alarm, she picked a tweed skirt, a waistcoat and a cheesecloth blouse. The only thing that I liked about the outfit was the cowboy boots that she chose to go with it. I looked at myself in the mirror for a long time, unable to recognise the girl who was looking back at me. I think she was shopping with herself in mind, but I didn't care. Spending time with Kate without the other girls was special to me. I didn't know why, exactly, all I knew was that my relationship with her felt different.

On St Patrick's Day, I came downstairs in my new clothes. 'Ta-dah!' I announced to my family in the kitchen. My mam's eyes opened wide with delight. 'Well, don't you look lovely!' She'd finally got the girl in the dress that she'd always longed for. Dad didn't know where to look, because this was so out of character for me, but my sister said I looked beautiful. This was not a word I'd ever heard said about me and I skipped out of the door on a high. Before I got to the front gate, Mam came running down the path with my black shoulder bag, which had never been used once since my Confirmation. She placed it on my shoulder, giving me a kiss on the cheek and the biggest hug, leaving me breathless for a moment. With tears in her eyes, she said, 'Have a wonderful day.'

'I love you, Mam,' I replied.

My heart was full of joy. I felt good and I told myself I looked even better. My waistcoat was covering the horrible boobs that seemed just to keep growing and my skirt made me feel sophisticated.

As I walked to Todd's department store, a Limerick landmark where I'd arranged to meet the girls, I felt a million dollars. The place was packed with people, a lot of whom were staring at me. For once it didn't bother me – sure, wasn't I beautiful in my new clothes with a big smile on my face? When I caught sight of the girls, I noticed the looks of surprise on their faces. I didn't know whether they were impressed or not, but one by one they told me how good I looked.

'I got something for you,' Kate said, taking a tweed cap from her bag, which she placed on my head. 'It completes your new look,' she said with a big warm smile.

We linked arms and walked to find a good vantage point to watch the parade. It seemed like the whole of Limerick was in the city. The sun was shining and I was having a wonderful day. As the parade came to an end, we decided to head to the Potato Market to get some lemonade to finish off the day. Just as we got to the market, some of my old friends from school saw us and came up to us. I was happy to see them, if only to show off my new clothes and introduce them to my new friends.

I wasn't prepared for the reaction I got. When I got close enough to hear them, one of them said, 'Will you look at Blackie O'Brien, dressed up like a dog's dinner with her posh friends.' One of them pulled the cap from my head and started to pass it around amongst themselves. When I tried to get it back, the laughter just got louder and more people joined in. Looking at the fear and disgust in my new friends' eyes at what they were seeing, I couldn't hold back my tears any longer. Letting a roar of hate and the loudest 'fuck off' out of my mouth, I ran as fast as I could to get away from this horrible place.

I didn't stop until I got home, my lungs burning and my face tear-stained. I went to my bedroom and cried some more. I remember asking God, 'Why, why must my life be like this? Why can't people just let me be happy?' The memory of the gang passing my hat around and laughing at me, Blackie O'Brien, kept going around in my head.

Then I heard a soft knock on my bedroom door. 'Come in,' I said, trying to stop my tears.

Dad stuck his head around the door, then came in and sat on the bed. 'What's wrong?'

Through my tears, I told him. 'They were all calling me Blackie O'Brien and saying that I looked like a dog's dinner!'

He thought for a while then said, 'Dry your eyes, love,' he said, 'and come downstairs when you're ready.'

I took off my new clothes and rolled them in a ball, placed them in a black bag and swore never to wear them again. I put on my old, comfortable tracksuit that made me feel so much more like myself and I went downstairs to see where Dad was. He was in the back garden, hammering at something. As I came out the back door, he showed me his work, a long stick with a nail hammered into it, so that the sharp end poked out. It looked like something which could cause a lot of damage.

Saying nothing, Dad brought me back into the house, opened the front door and told me to sit on the stairs looking out onto the street. He sat beside me, then he handed me the stick. 'Go on out the door and find the people who hurt you.' Pointing at my forehead, he told me to hit them as hard as I could with the stick.

I got up and walked to the door. I stood there, looking back at Dad sitting on the stairs. Eventually, I said, 'Their parents will kill me if I do that.'

'Not to worry. I'll take care of them. Now, off you go,' he insisted.

I remembered a fight I'd once had with my friend Tommy and the way I'd hit out at him, almost breaking his jaw. Our friendship had ended pretty abruptly after that. The pain I felt about hurting him wasn't something I ever wanted to feel again and even though I had no love for my old school friends, I really didn't want to hurt them in this way.

I took one more step and with tears in my eyes, I turned back to Dad. Dad stood up, took the stick from my hand and closed the front door. We both sat back down on the stairs. Dad put his arms around me and said, 'Jacqueline, people are always going to have an opinion about who you are. Unfortunately, you will be called names because of the colour of your skin. Now, you can choose to fight these people all your life – because your colour will be with you until the day you die – or you can make something of your life. For you, not for them. They don't matter. You do.' He got up then, but before he went back into the kitchen, he added, 'Whatever you decide, I am right with you. Never forget whose daughter you are,' he said and he hugged me tightly.

That night, I went to bed, Dad's words ringing in my ears. 'Make something of your life.' *But how*, I wondered. *Who could I be if I was always Blackie O'Brien, the girl from the Mount. The girl who didn't belong anywhere.* It seemed that no matter how hard I tried, I would never be anyone else. *Dad was right*, I thought miserably.

The next day I was still upset. At breakfast time, Mam placed a big slice of apple tart on the table before me, complete with freshly whipped cream. 'There you go,' she said, 'your favourite, get it into you. I know you don't have breakfast, but eat up and don't mind what people have to say.' I had never eaten breakfast – a leftover habit from my days at the Mount – but I ate the tart hungrily, enjoying the taste of the apples and sweet pastry. Then I decided to take my anger out on the bags of spuds and briquettes that waited for me, loading the shed for Dad's shop in double-quick time.

Still angry, I went to the park, did a few laps and kicked the ball around. As I ran, I decided I could never show my face again in the pool hall. The fear on my new friend's faces when they'd met my old gang told me they wouldn't want a friendship with someone like me. And my old friends had called them posh bastards from the rich part of town. That was it, I decided as I ran. I'd stay on my side of town. Maybe one day I'd make something of myself like Dad said, but in the meantime, I'd keep my head down.

After my run, I finished all my jobs around the shop and went to my room to read some poetry that Dad had written. We both loved to read and even though I was dyslexic, focusing on reading stopped me from overthinking. I could get lost in a book and look up to find that hours had passed.

To my surprise at four o'clock Mam called up the stairs for me to come down. 'Jackie? There are some people here to see you.' I thought it must be some of the girls from my soccer team letting me know what time our match was on later that night. I went slowly downstairs but when I reached the hall, my heart almost stopped. There at the open front door were my friends from the posh side of town. I couldn't believe my eyes. I felt like crying but I wouldn't let them see me do that. They had come across to Kileely to see me – to my part of town.

'So, these are the girls I've been hearing about,' Mam said, joining me on the front step. 'Lovely to meet you, girls. Now, go into the shop and get yourselves an ice cream.' My friends were dead impressed that my parents owned a shop and after we'd dug around in the freezer and picked what we wanted, I took them on a tour of my neighbourhood. Seeing it through their eyes, it wasn't the lovely suburb where they lived, but everyone stopped to say hello and kids raced around everywhere. 'This is great!' one of the girls exclaimed. *Funny*, I thought, *I never really thought of it in that way*. As home. After the grand tour, I picked up my soccer boots and we all headed to Shelbourne Park for my match. I played a blinder, scoring three goals. My head had never been higher.

CHAPTER 7

ENDGAME

Over the next few weeks, I began to see a lot more of Kate. The other three girls got summer jobs, and so it was just the two of us. We seemed to go everywhere together and she even invited me to dinner at her house, which to me was a big deal. Her mam was lovely and I loved the way she called me 'Jacqueline', as if I were her equal. I felt so much at home. I knew that the summer wouldn't last forever and that soon the girls would be back at school, but I was determined to make the most of it.

After the Shelbourne Park match, I had been offered the chance of playing on a factory team in Shannon, EI Electronics: all I had to do was wait until I reached 16 at the end of the year. Meanwhile, Kate and I became inseparable. We spent so much of our time together that summer of 1977, rambling around the city, talking, eating ice cream, heading to Donkey Ford's, a local chipper and Limerick institution. When Kate wasn't around, I noticed that I began to miss her more. I often found myself wondering where she was at any given moment. I wondered how her day was going and if she missed me. At night, I found myself dreaming of her, thinking that we'd go on holidays together and I'd spend as much time as I could with her.

I soon realised that this was getting out of hand but I didn't understand it.

Once, I'd played a match for Limerick against Dublin. Even though they were by far the stronger team, I was full of confidence on the soccer pitch and I had no fear of any other player, even though some of the opposition had been part of the first Irish international team in 1973. Even though I was skinny, I was tall and fast and I had good skills with my feet and in the air.

In the first half of the match, I was speeding up the field when I was faced with one of the Dublin defenders. I made my way around her and went on to score. As we came off the pitch, I was elated. Then someone tugged at my jersey and I looked around to see the furious face of the Dublin player. With a look that could kill, she hissed, 'I'll get you in the second half.' Another player then pushed into me and said furiously, 'I'll be looking out for you.' I was terrified when I got back into the dressing room. I couldn't understand it: Dublin were 6-1 up to us at this point, I told the girls on my team, so what was the problem?

They all roared with laughter and one of them said 'Don't worry. It's because you got made an Irish international and her girlfriend is mad with you.'

I was so puzzled by the 'international' remark that it took a while for the 'girlfriend' to sink in. *What's she talking about*, I thought. Girls don't have girlfriends; they have boyfriends. I can remember suddenly feeling sick to my stomach. I rushed out of the changing room and told the manager that I was feeling unwell and couldn't play the second half. All the way home, I prayed for the two girls in the sinful relationship. I'd been raised a Catholic and I knew that it was a sin for one girl to love another.

I had only the smallest inkling that that was the way I felt or was beginning to feel. At the time, I had hardly any understanding of being gay, but at the same time, something inside me was beginning to form. It would take many years before it came out into the open.

Every Friday night, all four of us girls would go to the cinema to see our favourite horror movies. We'd all sit in a row and watch a Hammer House of Horror, with Peter Cushing and Christopher Lee, loving every scary moment. During the scariest parts, Kate would move closer to me, letting out a scream and burying her head in my chest. I would automatically wrap my arms around her in a protective way. It was innocent, but inside, I thought, *God, what's going on? Why is my heart beating so fast?* It wasn't as if I was scared of the movie. It was having Kate in my arms that was making me feel this way. I'd quickly pull my arms back and sit up straight, laughing off what had just happened.

One Friday night, Kate had reached for my hand and squeezed it during the scary bits and my heart began to pound in my chest. This time, after we headed to Donkey Ford's for some chips, I found I couldn't eat mine. I had lost my appetite completely. I suddenly just wanted to go home, so I said goodbye to the girls, ignoring their looks of concern. 'I'll see you in Chalk and Cue on Sunday,' I said.

As I walked over Thomond Bridge, the Shannon speeding beneath me, I could see the square shape of St Munchin's Church in front of me. I decided I needed to talk to God. I sat on a bench beside the famous Treaty Stone, marking the city's surrender to William of Orange, and looked into the churchyard. I asked God what was happening to me. Why was I feeling this way?

I asked him why I couldn't get Kate out of my head. I remembered the two girls from the Dublin soccer team who were in a relationship. *Oh, my God*, I thought, *I'm one of them. I can't be. I'm a good person but people like that go to hell*, I thought. Gays. I knew that for a fact.

I was gay.

With the sin of loving Kate weighing heavily on my soul, I walked slowly home to my bed. But sleep wouldn't come to me that night. I thought of my mam and dad; the shame I would bring to them if anyone found out. *People would stop coming into the shop*, I thought. Dad might go back on the drink. My sisters and brother would be laughed at and made fun of and God knows, I knew what that felt like. The finger-pointing and the staring would become their lives now. I just couldn't do that to them.

By the time morning came, I knew what I had to do.

It was a Saturday, so I cleaned up my little shop and opened it up for the weekend. I would take orders in the morning for chickens then I would kill and pluck them for the customers to pick up later that evening. I've never been squeamish about this kind of thing, after all, I was used to it, and chicken at the time was a big treat for families. But this time, I found that my hands were shaking and it was hard to do the job. I began to feel sorry for the poor creatures, holding them gently in my hands, feeling their hearts beating rapidly. Still, I persisted and when it was time for Mam and Dad to close the main shop, I told them I'd do it. 'You go on home,' I said to them. 'I'll lock up.'

Delighted, Mam and Dad retreated into the house to catch the end of the Saturday film on TV. My plan was finally falling into place. At 11 o'clock, I locked up the shop, turned off the lights and went into the living room with the cash tin for Dad to count. 'Thanks, love,' Mam said and we settled in to watch the end of the movie. When it was over, I got up and went to the door to go to bed. Before I climbed the stairs, I turned around to look back at them both. 'Goodnight. I love you.' I wasn't normally this forthcoming, so Mam and Dad looked a bit surprised, but they both smiled warmly, as did I. But as I closed the door behind me and walked up the stairs, the tears started to flow. I went to my sisters' room and kissed them on the head, as they were both fast asleep in happy dreamland. Then, I went into my room, where Gerard was also fast asleep. I tossed his hair as I did so often and placed a kiss on the top of his head without waking him. With my goodbyes said, I took out the pack of 20 paracetamol from my pocket and stuffed them into my mouth. I washed them down with a bottle of cream soda, a mix of sweetness and bitterness filling my mouth. I'd bought two packets of painkillers but thought that one would probably be enough.

I lay in the dark and thought about Kate. I hadn't said goodbye to her, but it was too late now, I thought as my eyes began to close. I wasn't sure if it was the effects of the painkillers or the previous night's lack of sleep, but I began to feel drowsy, my scalp tingling. As I closed my eyes, I said to God, 'I'm ready for my punishment. Do as you will.'

To my horror, I woke up the next morning. Mam was leaning over me shaking my shoulders. 'Jackie, get up! You've slept in and you need to open the shop.' My first thought was, *for fuck's sake, I didn't take enough.* My head was hurting but I was still alive. I couldn't believe it.

When I went downstairs, Mam said, 'You look terrible.'

'I don't feel very well,' I admitted. My face was pale and I had deep black bags under my eyes.

'Go back to bed and I'll do the shop for you today: just this one time, mind,' Mam said.

Gratefully, I went back up the stairs to my room. Gerard was awake, bouncing up and down in his little bed. 'Is it time to get up now?' he said.

'Why don't you go and wake your sisters up?' I said to him. I wanted him out of the room, because I didn't want him to see me take the second packet of paracetamol. Next thing, I remember waking up to the sound of my sisters and brother making noise and laughing downstairs in the sitting room. The packet of Anadin was on the bed beside me. I hadn't taken them. I must have fallen asleep before I got the chance. I was so annoyed with myself: *I couldn't even get this right*, I thought. I snatched the packet up and emptied it into my hand, shovelling the twenty tablets into my mouth and swallowing them down. I had to get it right this time.

Then came a moment of clarity. God hadn't taken me because I hadn't said goodbye to my friends and especially to Kate. I had to get to the pool hall as quickly as I could, I decided, before the second pack of tablets did the trick. Don't ask me how I did it, but I managed to get out of the house and into town without falling over or getting sick, even though my stomach threatened to empty itself a few times on the way. I had a hard time getting up the stairs of the pool hall as my legs were now heavy and my head was swaying from side to side.

I got in the door and with my now-blurred eyesight, I could just about make out my friends. I made my way over to them, bumping into other people on the way. I could hear voices saying 'Jackie? Are you drunk?' I couldn't answer them, as my mouth wouldn't open to make any words and as I reached my friends, I collapsed on the floor. I just wanted to close my eyes and go to sleep but all I could hear was someone urging me to stay awake and my face being slapped. Then I could feel my body being lifted into the air, as if I was floating. God, where was I? Is this what happens when you die? I wondered. Was I floating out of my body? Then it went dark.

Next thing, I could hear a beeping noise and a man's voice in my ear asking me what I had taken. *How come God didn't know?* I thought hazily. *Wasn't he all-seeing and all-hearing?* I could feel that I was in a vehicle of some kind and then there was a very bright light and I realised that I wasn't in heaven. I was in hospital. A doctor appeared beside me with a syringe containing a dark fluid and a length of pipe. 'We're going to have to flush out the drugs,' he said. They had found the empty packets in my pocket. As they pushed the tube down my throat, I heard a nurse say gently, 'Your parents are outside.' *God, please let me die*, I thought. *I can't face them or tell them the truth.*

My thoughts continued to torture me as the fluid made its way into my stomach and I began to gag. Not only did Mam not get back her little girl when I'd come home all those years ago, but now, she'd got back a monster. She just didn't deserve this. *She should have left me in the industrial school with the nuns and this wouldn't have happened*, I thought miserably. *If she'd left me there, everyone would have been much better off.*

After the horrible ordeal of having my stomach pumped, I felt empty and shaken. I lay on the trolley in the cubicle in A&E while Mam and Dad were let in to see me. The look of fear on both their faces said it all. I'll never forget it. Mam sat on the side of the bed and held my hand. 'How are you feeling?' she asked me.

Dad paced up and down, looking grim, before finally asking, 'Look, has someone done something to you, Jackie? Tell me who it was,' he said, adopting his usual role of my protector.

The lie I told them came quickly into my head. 'I just had a terrible, ehrm, headache, so I took some Anadin,' I said. 'Then the next day, my headache was worse, so I took some more. I'm sorry, I should have asked Mam what to do, but Dad was around and I was too embarrassed to say anything . . .'

I could see from the look of relief on both their faces that they believed my lie. When the doctor came back in, he asked Mam if there was any reason I might have taken so many painkillers. 'Period pains,' Mam said quietly. Dad looked embarrassed.

'Well, maybe you might have a chat about the time of the month,' the doctor said, looking sceptical.

'Thank you, doctor,' Mam said. She turned to me. 'The next time you have tummy cramps, tell me. I'll get you a hot water bottle.' Then she began to cry, tears running down her face. *She knows*, I thought.

'She's one strong cookie,' the doctor said. 'She should have no after-effects, other than a sore throat and one hell of a headache.' He added that they'd monitor me for the night and let me go home in the morning.

Mam and Dad kissed me on the top of my head and said goodnight. As my eyes closed, I fell into a deep sleep. The following day, no questions were asked by Mam or the doctor. As far as I was concerned, my lie had worked. When we got home, I got big hugs from my sisters and brother: I hadn't realised that they missed me so much, but then, I suppose they'd never really been without me. I wondered then if I meant more to them than I'd thought.

'Off you go to bed,' Mam said to me. 'You need to rest.'

This time, rest didn't come to me. Apart from the embarrassment of what happened in the pool hall, I reasoned that I still was going to hell for having feelings about my friend, Kate. What could I do? *I can't try to kill myself again*, I thought. I saw the pain I had caused Mam and Dad. *No*, I decided, *I'll just have to stay away from the pool hall until I figure out what to do.*

There was only one person I could turn to – Rita Spring, my old school teacher from Ballynanty. We'd stayed in touch since I'd left school and I'd often pop in for a chat. She wrote letters to me from her native Kerry when she went home for the holidays. The letters were full of wonderful stories about her family and her life on the farm and I really treasured them. I could confide in her, I knew.

Two days later, I made my way up to the school and found Rita in the staff room, chatting with one of the nuns. Even though I hadn't been in that nun's class, she'd always been so nice to me whenever we'd met in the hallway. When they caught sight of me, big smiles broke out on both their faces. 'Jackie!' Rita exclaimed. 'It's so good to see you.'

At this, my tears started to flow.

'Oh dear,' Rita said, 'sit down here Jackie and tell me what the matter is.' The nun went to put the kettle on. Within minutes,

I was off. I offloaded all my guilt about my feelings for Kate, my suicide attempt, the difficulties I had fitting in. With the nun there, it felt a little like Confession. After all, she had a hotline to God, I reasoned as I unburdened myself. When I had finished, I looked from one to the other, expecting condemnation or judgement. Instead, Rita took both my hands in hers and said, 'Jacqueline, don't you know God loves you? He made you just as you are. Why would he not love you? He would want you to live and love whoever was lucky enough to come into your life.'

I looked at the nun for reassurance and she nodded in agreement. I couldn't believe it.

'Have you told your friends how you've been feeling?' Rita asked.

'I can't,' I replied. I could never tell Kate, as I knew she liked boys, which I had seen from our Sundays at the disco. I couldn't stand the pain of losing her friendship too.

With my hands still in hers, Rita asked, 'What are you good at?'

'Soccer,' I said immediately.

With a big smile on her face Rita said, 'Well, why don't you concentrate on your football and go and make the Irish team?' I looked at her as if she were mad. I was good but me on the Irish team? *You must be joking.* 'Well, I've been offered this job in Shannon,' I told them, 'because of my soccer.'

'Well, if you're good enough to be offered a job on the strength of your soccer, with some hard work, you could make the Irish team,' Rita said.

I'd never thought about soccer in those terms before. That apart from being something I loved, it could be part of my plans for my future. That I, a girl from an industrial school, could one day play for my country. It was scary and exciting at the same time. What's more, I thought, as I sat on the bus home from Ballynanty, when it came to telling the girls what had happened, I could stick to my story about having period pains. As I looked out the window at the streets of Limerick passing by, I kept repeating, 'God loves me. I'll play for Ireland. God loves me, I'll play for Ireland . . .'

Feeling so much lighter, I had only one more thing to do. One Sunday afternoon, I plucked up the courage to go to John's Pavilion to the disco to see my friends. The last time I'd seen them, I'd been incoherent, collapsing on the floor. As I walked in, I was shaking like a leaf, but when my friends caught sight of me, they ran over to me, clearly delighted to see me.

'My God, Jackie, are you all right?' one of them said. 'We were really worried about you.'

I shrugged. 'Oh, it was just period pain.' I retold my lie, which by this stage, I was starting to believe myself. 'I took one too many Anadin for the cramps.' They were all ears when I got to the part about the long tube and the syringe to make me vomit the tablets I had taken. With my story told I looked on the dance floor to see Kate in a loving embrace with the young man she had spoken about a few times. As the dance came to an end, she caught sight of me and ran over, hugging me and saying how good it was to see me. Then she turned to her boyfriend and introduced me. Even though I knew that Kate liked boys, I was heartbroken. But in that moment, I knew she was happy and that I had to be happy for her.

Then, looking over my shoulder, she smiled and said, 'I think you have an admirer.'

I turned around to see a guy with the biggest head of afro hair and the widest smile on his face. That was the day I met Christy Higgins and we became lifelong friends. It was time for me to forget my unhealthy thoughts for my friend. To bury them forever. The words kept playing in my head: 'God loves me. Go play for Ireland'.

Over the next few weeks, I stopped going to the pool hall. Instead, I went training on my own in the park. I continued to go to the Sunday disco and I would meet Kate and my friends but things were never the same between Kate and me, at least, not for me anyway. She had her boyfriend and I was happy for her and besides, I now had Christy.

One Sunday, he walked up to me and placed a bar of chocolate and an apple in my hand. 'I thought you might like this,' he said. I remember thinking, *how nice is that*? Later, when a slow dance came on, he asked me to dance with him. I felt awkward as he put his arms around my waist. I didn't know where to put my hands. Looking over at my friends for guidance they gestured for me to put my hands on his shoulders, which I shyly did. After that day, Christy and I would often meet in town. We'd go to the pictures and wander around town with his friends, but even though we loved each other, there was no way sex would be a thing. I was only 16 and I was very uncomfortable talking about sex or even talking to my friends about it. As a Black child growing up in Limerick, I was seen as 'exotic', a word I came to hate over the years because of its implications for me. On many occasions, grown men would make sexual advances towards me: grabbing my breasts or backside. Once, when I was travelling on a bus, it stopped and, with me the only passenger on board, the driver left his seat and came and sat beside me. 'How about a little kiss?' he said.

'No, thank you,' I said, terrified.

He then proceeded to try and put his hands down my pants. Thankfully, I was strong enough to fight him off, and when the conductor got back on the bus after a cigarette break, he yelled at the driver to leave me alone. The driver thought it was funny. 'I'm only having a bit of fun with the pretty little thing.' It wasn't fun for me.

This incident would have a huge bearing on my life. I learned that sex was something dirty and wrong and what's more, it had happened to me because of my colour. I never told a soul about that afternoon, but I carried the lessons with me into my life.

CHAPTER 8

RUNNING HOME

The idea came to me slowly. It was 1977 and I was 16 years old. I had put my overdose and unrequited love for Kate into a box, which I would store neatly away somewhere in my head. I didn't want to remember how desperate I was, how close I'd come to ending it all. I wasn't ready to deal with it, or to look more closely at what might have got me to that point.

For me, being from Limerick and growing up there, was a real mixture of happiness and heartbreak. I had the toughest of all starts, but my parents had tried their very best to make up for that when I joined the family as a little girl. They'd provided me with a strong framework of morals, values and a fair dose of Catholic guilt, pretty much like every Irish person at the time. But I've often wondered whether it's possible to ever fully put those early years behind me. They were my formative years and I'd spent them without love and comfort, feeling a sense of shame and guilt that, now that I look back on it, had nothing to do with me. But that didn't matter. I felt them anyway.

I also felt a longing to know who I truly was. I loved my city, but I was tired of the stares and the pointing, the 'jokes' about my skin colour. I had developed the habit of making the jokes myself before others could. In a crowded disco, I'd say 'Jesus, it's Black in here,' and so on, but it came at a cost to myself. I felt the loneliness of always being the only one and what it was like to be different. Even Mam and Dad didn't understand my sadness about having no-one in my life who looked like me, who shared my heritage.

I'd taken to asking my mother about my biological father, firing questions at her about who he was. She would always get upset and say, 'Jackie, Mickey O'Brien is your dad. That's all you need to know.' She was right. Mickey O'Brien was my dad, but still, he wasn't my father.

The more I pushed for an answer, the more our relationship suffered. I think she was hurt that I'd even ask about a dad I'd never met, but even while I felt guilty about being disloyal to the man who had been the only dad I knew, the need to know more about how I came to be was stronger.

Then I had an idea. I'd run away to Birmingham to find out the answers to my questions for myself. I was working in EI Electronics in Shannon, while playing on the company soccer team. I saved my wages and made a plan to buy a ferry ticket to Holyhead, which was a lot of money at the time, then I'd take the train to Birmingham. I confided in one of my friends in EI, Liz, who thought it would be a great adventure and asked if she could come with me. I was delighted: I'd never been out of Limerick and I was scared about the prospect of going to Birmingham on my own.

During the weeks that followed this plan, I scrimped and saved, knowing that in a few weeks' time I'd be leaving Limerick forever. My plan was that if I found my real father and it worked out, I'd stay in Birmingham and leave the mess and complications of my life in Limerick behind. Liz and I set the date for our departure, but before that, I'd have one last night in my new favourite place, Shannon Rugby Club, to say goodbye. Some of the boys I played soccer on the road with were also at the club and when they heard my plans, they urged me to go up to the DJ and ask for a special song to be played to wish me luck. It was as if I was emigrating, which I was, in a way. I was over the moon and took it as a sign that I was doing the right thing.

Before I left the disco that night, I bumped into an ex of one of the Kileely boys, a girl called Siobhan. 'Jackie, I haven't seen you in ages!' she exclaimed.

'I know. How's the baby?' I asked her. I knew that Siobhan was a single mum to a newborn girl.

'She's fabulous,' she said. 'Did you know I called her Jackie?' I thought this was amazing: the idea that someone thought so highly of me that they'd call their baby after me. 'Listen, will you come over to mine for a cup of tea?' she asked. 'You can say hello to the other Jackie.'

I was so glad of the invitation and told Liz I'd make my way to the station in the morning to meet her there. I hadn't breathed a word of my plans to anyone other than Liz. As far as Mam and Dad were concerned, I was staying in Liz's house in Ballynanty and would be back home the following day.

We caught a cab back to Siobhan's house in Fairgreen and she introduced me to her Mum, Mary and we all three sat chatting for the next hour or so. When Mary announced she was going to bed, I got up to leave. 'No, it's far too late for you to go looking for a cab, Jackie,' Mary said. 'Do your Mam and Dad know where you are? I'm sure they'd be worried about you being out so late.'

'Well, I was supposed to stay in a friend's house,' I said, 'but we got separated at the disco.' It wasn't a lie.

'In that case, I'd feel happier if you'd stay here,' she said. 'I'll sleep easier knowing that you're safe.'

When Mary went up the stairs, Siobhan and I put the kettle back on and we both sat in the sitting room chatting all night. I had never sat and talked to anyone so openly and honestly about life and its ups and downs, about my rocky relationship with Mam – it felt great to let my fear and worries out. That night, a lifelong friendship was formed.

As I left the following morning, Siobhan said, 'Look, if things don't work out in Birmingham, there'll always be a place for you here.' I was overwhelmed by her generosity and by the way in which she'd listened to me. She has been my friend and confidante ever since.

I'd arranged to meet Liz at the train station at 7 o'clock the following morning to catch a bus to the ferry in Dublin. As we loaded our two suitcases on the bus, I was full of joy and excitement but also sadness. Mam and Dad didn't have any idea that I was running away. I knew that they'd both be hurt, but my need to know was so great, I pushed my sadness aside. I was becoming really good at blocking out things that caused me pain. It would become a lifelong pattern.

The bus ride to Dublin seemed to take forever, but when I caught sight of the ship, the excitement began to mount. I'd never seen anything like it before, a huge white passenger ferry being filled with cars and lorries. Would the ship not sink from all that weight, I wondered. What if there weren't enough lifeboats or jackets for all the people on board. I began to panic as visions of the *Titanic* filled my mind. *Maybe it wasn't worth it to find a man who probably hadn't wanted me*, I began to think. After all, he hadn't married my mam. But as soon as I had the thought, I realised that it did matter – to me.

Once on board the ship I marvelled at the bar and restaurant and with our savings, Liz and I tucked into a huge meal. Probably not the best idea, given the seasickness that followed. We were so innocent. When two young men took a shine to Liz and came and sat at our booth, we let them chat away to us, loving their English accents. After a while, they moved a little too close for our liking and started to put their arms around us and ask for a kiss. Liz and I felt very uncomfortable and started to look around trying to catch the eye of one of the older passengers for some help, before nature intervened. My stomach started to twist, I jumped up and beckoned to Liz that I was going to be sick. We both ran to the nearest bathroom, and by the time we emerged, the English guys had long gone. At least we'd gotten rid of them, I thought wearily as I slumped onto the table in our little booth.

I can't remember how long we were on the ship but it seemed like a lifetime since we'd left the train station in Limerick. The excitement had started to fade and I would have given anything to be back in my bedroom at home with my sisters and my little brother. Liz did her best to cheer me up: 'Remember, it'll all be worth it to meet your dad.'

The first thought I had when we took our seats on the train to Birmingham was that this was going to be a lot harder than we thought. There were so many Black people on the train that I thought, surely this was Africa, not England. In my head I thought all I had to do was go to Birmingham and that the first man walking down the road would be my father. All I had to do was to find him. Now, I realised that far from being one of a handful of Black people I knew, I was in a country full of them. This might sound naïve, but I was a very innocent girl who had never been outside my little corner of the world. Everything was a surprise to me.

When the train pulled into Birmingham's New Street station, my excitement began to grow again. We clambered down from the train and found our way to the Bullring. We stood in the expanse of concrete that was the city's landmark and I remembered that I'd heard Mam and Auntie Joan talking about it. Now, I was finally here and it was time to put the next part of my plan into action. I knew that my mam's other sister, Marie, lived in Kings Heath and that she worked in Tesco's. I was going to find her first.

We needed to ask directions and overwhelmed by all of the different cultures, I insisted that we only ask white people: in my naïveté, I thought that the Black people wouldn't understand us. Maybe they didn't speak English, I thought. I didn't think that I was like them in many ways. While my hair was curly, it was soft and my skin was paler. I found myself scanning their features to see if they resembled mine in the shape of their eyes or noses. I was surrounded by Africans, West Indians, people from Pakistan and South Asia: *which one of these groups belongs to me*? I wondered.

As if she read my mind, Liz said, 'I wonder if your dad would look the same as you?'

How would I know? I worried.

Looking back, it must have been quite funny for people watching two little Irish girls struggling with two huge suitcases into Tesco's. I told Liz to stay at the entrance and mind our bags while I went and got my aunt. I had never met her in person: all she was to me was a photo in the living room of our home in Limerick. So, after walking up and down the aisles a few times, I saw no sign of her. Then a very kind lady working in the shop approached me and asked if she could help me.

'My name is Jacqueline O'Brien,' I said to her. 'I'm looking for my aunt, Marie O'Halloran.'

She looked puzzled. 'Nobody of that name works here, love.'

My heart sank.

'Does she work in another branch?' she asked me gently.

I shook my head, a tight knot in my stomach. 'She definitely works in Tesco's in Kings Heath.'

'Oh,' she brightened. 'Are you from Ireland? There's a Marie Flynn here who is originally from Ireland.' Of course, silly me. Marie's maiden name was O'Halloran but her husband was John Flynn. 'Let's go and see,' she said, leading me to the storeroom at the back of the shop. After a few minutes, she returned with another woman, who looked puzzled when she saw me. 'What can I do for you, pet?'

She doesn't look like the woman in the photo at home, I thought. Maybe she wasn't Auntie Marie at all. But then she smiled and it was unmistakable. Her smile was exactly the same as Mam's.

I took a step towards her and smiled, saying, 'It's me, Auntie Marie, it's Jacqueline O'Brien.'

The look of shock, as the realisation of who this stranger was kicked in, was one I will never forget. She looked behind me and asked, 'Where's your mother?' as if she were expecting her sister to appear at any moment, shouting 'surprise!'

'She's at home in Limerick. I've come with a friend.'

'Does your mother know that you're here?' she said sharply.

I shook my head and whispered, 'No'.

Instead of the warm embrace which I had imagined, she gave me a look that could kill, grabbed me by the arm and pulled me to the front desk. 'I'm taking my dinner break,' she told the woman on the front till. Then she marched Liz and I up the road, pulling our bags behind us. All the way, she gave out to me about what I must be putting my poor mother and father through and didn't I think I was causing enough trouble and so on. *Thank God it's not far*, I thought, as my ear was about to fall off with the blistering lecture she was giving me.

Once inside the house, Liz and I were shown into the sitting room, but before my backside could reach the couch, I was once again caught by the ear and brought into the hallway. Marie sat me down on a little stool beside the hall table, on which stood a phone. With murder still in her eyes, she picked up the receiver and proceeded to dial a number. She placed the receiver into my hand and barked, 'Talk'.

I hadn't a clue who she had called, but a second later my heart sank. 'Is that you, Jacqueline?' It was Mam. I knew immediately the pain and worry I'd caused her. It was in her voice.

'I just wanted to see the country I was born in,' I said to her. 'And maybe play a bit of soccer while I'm here,' I added, as if that would reassure her. I mentioned nothing about trying to find

72

my birth father. She listened, then said wearily, 'Put me back on to your auntie.'

I returned to the sitting room, where Liz was waiting anxiously. The colour must have drained from my face as I sat down on the sofa. When Marie came back into the room, clearly about to give me another earful, she said, 'Are you all right?'

'I feel sick,' I said. It wasn't a lie, but it wasn't my stomach this time, it was my heart.

Marie's expression softened. 'Come on upstairs and lie down for a bit. You look exhausted. We'll talk later,' she added ominously.

I don't think my head hit the pillow before my eyes and body seemed to just shut down. When I woke up, it took me a few minutes to figure out where I was. I could hear laughter coming from downstairs and hoped it would continue when I went down to face the music. When I entered the sitting room, I was so relieved. Auntie Marie gave me a big smile and I was relieved to see the murderous look in her eyes had been replaced with one of warmth. Liz was chatting with John Flynn, my uncle, and to the brightest 13-year-old girl, my cousin Helena. I had never met my uncle or cousins before, so I was quite shy. Thank God for Helena, though, as she could talk for Ireland and she came at me with a hundred questions, which I tried to answer.

'You sound just like Phil Lynott,' she said. 'It's your accent and you look like him, too. When you came in, I thought, ohmygod, you must be his sister.' Then the questions came: 'Do you know where he lives?' 'Do you live near him?' 'Have you ever seen him?'

'Leave your cousin alone,' Auntie Marie said. 'You can ask all the questions you want later. I need to talk to her.' She brought me into the kitchen and sat me down at the table, sitting opposite me, her arms crossed. 'Now, you were very wrong to run away and upset your mam and dad like that.'

'I know,' I said sadly.

'But I've spoken to your mother and she knows that you're safe here with me. You can stay here for a while and then we'll talk again to your parents.' Then, to my surprise, she reached over and gave me the biggest hug. Holding my face in her hands, she said, 'You've grown up so beautiful.' In that moment, I started to cry. Marie looked so much like Mam, it made me realise just how much I missed her.

Over the next few weeks, I got to know my auntie and my cousins, Pauline, David, Jonathan and Helena. They felt like family to me and I had a sense of belonging to them in a way I hadn't at home. I would walk to Tesco's to meet Auntie Marie after her work and she always introduced me to her colleagues with pride in her eyes. 'This is my sister Pat's child from Ireland.' No-one would bat an eyelid. There were no exclamations of wonder about my skin colour, or questions about how I could belong to this family. They just took it for granted that that's who I was. This was something new for me.

I soon began to settle into my new home. I loved the weekends in Birmingham. After a walk around the shops in Kings Heath and placing a few bets with my Uncle John, he would head to the Irish Club for a few beers, making sure that Liz and I had lemonade. *It's not as nice as Irish lemonade*, I thought, sipping it. Then we'd go back to the house for big platefuls of Marie's fabulous Irish stew. My favourite bit of the evening would be watching their giant TV, which seemed to have a hundred channels compared to our one or two in Ireland. I couldn't believe it and I loved channel hopping for the novelty. Then, at nine o'clock, Auntie Marie would get out a bottle of Jameson whiskey and a sing-song would start up. As she and Uncle John worked their way through all the well-known ballads, I would feel a wave of homesickness wash over me.

Of course, I didn't forget the reason why I'd come to Birmingham. I waited until I knew Marie a bit better, then one night, when everybody else was gone to bed, I asked her if she would tell me about my biological father.

With sadness in her eyes she sat me down. 'Look, it was hard for your mother when she found out that she was pregnant. Myself and John wanted to raise you as our own when you were born, to help your mother out.' She hesitated. 'Your mother hadn't told us who the father was, and I admit I got some fright when Pat turned up at the front door, soaking wet with a bundle in her arms.' She sighed. 'I can remember opening a drawer and stuffing it with a pillow to lay you on. I took you from your mother's arms and placed you in the little bed, then I pulled back the blanket to have a look at this new arrival.' She paused. 'I got the fright of my life, if I'm honest.'

Later on, I would learn what Marie said about the little monkey, but now, she explained to me that she hadn't wanted to hurt anyone with her comments. It was just that she wasn't expecting a black child and with the amount of hair I had on my head, it was the first thought that came to her mind. We both laughed at this. 'Your mother thought that it would be better for you to grow up in Ireland. Even in Birmingham, in 1961, it wasn't the done thing for a white woman to have a child with a black man.' As my grandad Josie had returned to Ireland in 1960 after a stint in Birmingham, Mam decided that if Grandad accepted her and me, she would return to Ireland with me.

'Your mother was so happy to be back in Ireland with you, you know,' Marie said. 'We'd send clothes over for you and do whatever else we could to help her, but until the day they came for you, Pat was happy with you and Josie. And, well, you know the rest. Pat told me that there was nothing she could do except run after the ambulance that was taking you away.'

Hearing this made me so sad but also so angry, not with Mam but with the nuns and not because of what they did to me but what they did to her. *How in the name of God could they be so cruel?* I thought. *What was it all for, only to take me away from her during the years that mattered the most?*

Seeing the sadness and anger in my eyes, Marie tried to lighten the tone. 'But look at the wonderful man she married and how hard they fought to get you back. They never gave up on you and they both love you so much.'

The anger left me and was replaced with shame for all I had put Mam and Dad through. They had done everything for me, and I'd repaid them by running away. What an ungrateful child I was. How could I ever face them again? Before I went to sleep that night, I promised myself that I would stop looking for the father who didn't want me in the first place and that I would make something of myself, to make Mam and Dad proud to call me their daughter.

I had no idea how to start looking for my father among all of the communities in Birmingham: it was long before Ancestry and other DNA sites and I lost heart at the scale of the challenge. Of course now, I understand that I wasn't an ungrateful, troublesome child. I was simply a naïve teenager looking for a place to belong.

A lot is written about trauma nowadays, but back then, it wasn't even acknowledged. Looking back, I can see that a lot of my behaviour at the time came out of that initial trauma of being taken away from my mother.

On the Friday night after my conversation with my auntie, I asked her if I could use the phone to call Ireland. She looked happy and said, 'Yes, of course, your mam and dad will be delighted to hear from you.'

It had been three weeks since I'd left Limerick for Birmingham and I had only spoken to Mam once. My shame and guilt were too strong for me to speak to my parents and so the number I dialled was for Shannon Rugby Club. This might sound a bit odd, but at the time, my friends were my world, and we'd all gather in the club on Saturday nights. It was there that I'd met Siobhan. *That's it*, I thought as I heard the ring tone. *I'll talk to Siobhan.*

In those days, every club and pub had a phone, generally in a little booth near the bar or on the way to the toilets. Calls would be picked up by anyone who happened to be passing and they'd fetch the person called to the phone. Now, I held the receiver to my ear as the phone rang for what seemed like forever. Just as I was going to give up, the phone was answered and I heard the best Limerick accent. When I said that it was me, the voice said, 'Well, kid, how's it going over there in the big smoke?'

'Ah, it's great.' The music was so loud, we both had to shout, so the guy said, 'hang on a minute.' The receiver dropped with a clunk, and after a few minutes I heard the music stop. Then, to my surprise, I heard the DJ announce, 'Jackie O'Brien is on the phone, so I'll stop the music and go have a cigarette and talk to her.'

I couldn't believe they stopped the music for me. Were they mad?

For the next ten minutes, I must have said the same thing a hundred times to everyone who crowded around the phone, asking me question after question. Yes, Birmingham was great. No, they didn't have Tayto and the lemonade was rubbish. I was told that the football team were missing me and had lost their last three matches. Finally, I said, 'Is Siobhan there?' I felt that I could be honest with her about my true feelings: that I was homesick for Limerick but didn't know how to come home without losing face. I felt trapped. She wasn't around and I put the phone down sadly.

How can I go home now? I thought. *After that big send-off in the rugby club? How can I face Mam and Dad?* There was no way I could just go home after everything that happened. But with no job to go back to, where would I live? Siobhan had offered me a bed but maybe she was just being nice. Why had I come here looking for a Black man who may or may not have been my father, I wondered. How foolish was I? The accusations to myself, the anger, swirled around in my head, but I couldn't make a decision.

Finally, Liz appeared in my room one afternoon and said that she wanted to go home, that she'd had enough. Just like that, I said, 'Right, I'm coming with you.' I had no idea what I'd face but anything was better than being here in limbo. We said our goodbyes and thank yous to Auntie Marie and Uncle John, who wished us a safe journey. 'Say hello to Pat for me,' Marie added. I felt a dart of shame and guilt then, because I hadn't told my parents that I was coming home. In truth, I had no idea what I was going home to.

CHAPTER 9

HOMECOMING

I got off the bus early one Saturday morning. In Limerick, the sky was grey and the pavements slick with rain. I could see the comforting outline of King John's Castle as I walked through the familiar streets that felt so quiet after the hustle and bustle of Birmingham. Liz and I said our goodbyes and then I was alone. No-one was coming to meet me, with my bags and suitcase. My only plan was to head to the rugby club that evening to surprise them with my return. The Prodigal Daughter. And then, out of the blue, Siobhan appeared. As I saw her walking down the street, I thanked God that Limerick was so small. I waved at her and she came over and gave me a hug, asking me a tonne of questions about Birmingham. When I explained my dilemma, she said, 'Come on back to my house and you can have a cup of tea while you decide.'

'So, how did it go in Birmingham?' she asked me now, linking my arm in hers as we walked to her house.

'Well, I couldn't find my dad at all,' I said. 'You've no idea how many people there are in Birmingham, let alone those who look like me.'

Siobhan nodded, encouraging me to go on. 'And you know what? If he didn't want me in the first place, I don't want him.

No,' I shook my head. 'I'm going to get a job and get back to playing soccer.'

Siobhan didn't say much: she just listened as I poured my heart out to her and when we got back to her house, I met her mam and her little baby girl, my namesake, Jackie. The previous time I'd met her, she'd been fast asleep in bed, but now she lay awake in her cot, gurgling and waving her little arms. I instantly fell in love with this tiny bundle. And when Mary, Siobhan's mother, invited me to stay in the spare room, I didn't hesitate. It offered me the perfect way out of having to face my parents. As if she read my mind, Mary said, 'Go off the two of you and enjoy your night out at the rugby club, but,' she added, looking at me intently, 'do me a favour and get in touch with your mam and dad and tell them at least that you're home.'

That night, I received a royal welcome at Shannon Rugby Club and when we got home, Siobhan and I talked all night. I offloaded everything that I couldn't tell my parents onto her and once again, she listened to it all. 'I can't go home, because I can't face them,' I told her, 'and all the pain I've caused them.' But mostly, I couldn't face Dad, this man who idolised me and had given me so much confidence in myself. 'At every corner, he was there and had my back, you know?' I told her. 'When I had to leave school because of my dyslexia, he saved me by giving me my own little shop to run. He defended me against racist comments, he encouraged my soccer.' I felt that looking for my biological father would be such a slap in the face for him. 'I just can't come to terms with that,' I told Siobhan.

'Maybe in time,' she said sympathetically.

I was grateful to Siobhan's mam Mary, but I was aware that she was a single mum and supporting the whole family, so I was pleased to get a job in St Joseph's Hospital to make my contribution. What's more, the job came with a place on the hospital soccer team. With my job and my very first paycheck, I cycled to Donkey Ford's chipper and I got the biggest takeaway I could manage. Battered sausages, fish and chips, you name it. I cycled back to Siobhan's in Fairgreen with my bounty. I can still remember laying the newspaper on the table, opening it out, all of us tucking in. We didn't even get plates: we just stuffed ourselves as if we hadn't eaten in weeks. It felt good to be able to repay Mary and Siobhan, even just with a takeaway.

I hadn't separated from my family completely, however. I would sneak into town to meet my younger sister, Regina, to get updates from home. I'd ask her how Dad was doing and if he'd gone back on the drink, but he hadn't, and Mam was doing okay and so was the shop. When she told me that Josie, my mam's father, was back, my heart stopped. It was Josie who had made it possible for my mother to return to Limerick with me as a baby. An electrician by trade, he had had to leave for England when I was still in the Mount, in search of work. Now, he was back and living with Mam and Dad. I was curious: Gina and Caroline and Gerard were my half-siblings, but Grandad Josie belonged fully to me.

At the same time, my friendship with Siobhan grew and I would say that I began to develop feelings towards her and especially towards Jackie, the baby. I loved them both and I sometimes used to think that if we ran away to England, we could be a little family. I felt that I wanted to look after them both, like the older girl had minded me in the Mount. I kidded myself that, with a haircut and my deep speaking voice, I could even pass for a man. But I also knew that, even though inside I was a little bit in love with Siobhan, our friendship mattered more to me.

I thought I'd stay with Siobhan and Mary forever, but in the end, it was to be almost two years. In those two years between 1978 and 1980, I went from being a naïve 17-year-old to a young woman with a job and a sporting career. I grew in confidence, but all the while I knew that something in me was unresolved.

'Would you not go and see your mam?' Siobhan said to me one day. It was as if she'd read my mind. Still, I was defensive.

'Why would you say that?' I asked her, taken aback.

Of course, Siobhan always knew what I was feeling even before I did. She had seen and understood my curiosity about home for what it was: a sign that I was ready to return. 'Look, your mam loves you,' she said. 'I don't think you're going to get turned away from the door. Apologise for what you've done and see what way the land lies.'

I hesitated and Siobhan pressed on. 'You can come back up here afterwards: just go and see.'

I thought about this for a long while. What would it mean to go home, to repair the relationship with Mam and Dad, I wondered. What would it be like to stop running away for a bit and work on what I had with my family? One evening after work, I jumped on the bus to Kileely.

Everything looked the same, I thought, as I got off the bus and walked around the corner into the warren of streets and houses that had been my home. I stood outside Mam and Dad's for a bit, looking at the house, at the shop attached to the side, and I wondered if I would have the courage to go in. Could I explain why I'd left for Birmingham in search of a man who didn't seem to exist? Would I spend my life chasing ghosts or would I choose what was right in front of me? I took a deep breath and went in.

Mam and Dad were behind the counter of the shop, as they usually were. On hearing the bell attached to the door they both looked up. I won't say I got the biggest smile, more of a look of curiosity from them both. Then Dad looked at Mam to gauge her reaction.

'Hi, Mam, how are you?' I said.

She just looked at me for a long time, before Dad said to me, 'Go on into the kitchen and put on the kettle on. Take a packet of biscuits from the shelf.'

I did as I was told, hands shaking as I lifted the kettle to the kitchen tap and emptied half a packet of biscuits onto a plate. Then Mam came in and we sat down around the table. There was silence, then I started to cry. It all came pouring out. 'I'm so sorry,' I told Mam. 'I know that you didn't want me to go to Birmingham, but I just wanted to know more about the other side of my family. Even if I met my father, I wouldn't have wanted to live with him. I only wanted to ask him why he didn't want me.'

Mam looked at me gently. 'I understand, Jackie, but you know, Mickey O'Brien has given both of us so much: a home, love, kindness and while he hasn't always been the greatest husband, he has always been a wonderful dad to you.' I knew and understood that, but when I'd left for Birmingham, Dad's love for me hadn't been the point. I felt that the issue was Mam's unwillingness to be more open about how I came to be. It was all shrouded in mystery and while she never said it, sometimes I felt that I'd ruined her plans for her exciting life in Birmingham, had thrown her off the path that she'd thought lay in front of her.

I never felt unloved by Mam but there were times when I just didn't like her and I know she didn't like me. I was tall and lanky – taller than Mam from the age of 12, and with my anger about everything that was unresolved between us, I must have been intimidating to her. Any row that we had, I would keep it going for days on end, not talking to her, slamming doors, being unwilling to back down when she wouldn't tell me what I wanted to know. I also knew my relationship with Dad, stronger than my relationship with Mam, made her angry. I could see her thinking, *how is it she goes along with everything he says and ignores me?* I was her child after all. I think that Mam felt a sense of guilt about those missing years and that by coming home to Limerick, she'd set in train my future in the Mount.

I understood that I'd resented Mam. I often thought that if she had left me in Birmingham or had me adopted, maybe I would have grown up with a Black family and been able to be myself. I wouldn't have gone to the Mount and endured all the pain that followed.

Even though we sat together for an hour, I think we both knew that there was a lot going on under the surface that we didn't have the language for. We weren't the kind of people who could talk about our feelings, at least, not yet. And so, we reached a kind of a truce. I remembered how lonely I'd felt in Birmingham without Mam and Dad and my brother and sisters and I knew that I'd have to let my quest for my real father go. I remember thinking, *I'll figure it out in Ireland. I'm Irish and I'll work it out at home.* My Irishness was not in doubt while the other side of my heritage was a mystery to me. I had no idea where my father even came from: India, Africa, the West Indies. *Where will I even start to look*, I wondered.

Over the next few weeks, I would come and go between Siobhan's and Mam and Dad's, before eventually one day, Mam said, 'Why don't you just move home? Your room is there for you.'

The time seemed right. I went back and told Siobhan I was moving home. 'I'm delighted for you. I really am,' she said, pulling me into a big hug. There were tears in both our eyes. We'd shared so much together but I knew that we'd be friends forever.

At home in Kileely, life resumed pretty much as it had been before I'd left for Birmingham. I got to know Grandad Josie, the man who'd helped my mother back in those early days; a storyteller with a huge mop of hair, he loved to go to the pub and regale the locals. I started to help out in the shop again, driving Dad's car to the cash and carry to get supplies for the shop. I was quite a competent driver at this point, and I've always loved cars. I longed to have my own, and one day, I came home from work to find a beautiful blue Toyota Corolla in the driveway. When I walked into the living room, Dad was holding a set of keys in his hand. 'It's for you,' he said, smiling, handing me the keys. I fell in love with that car immediately: it had leather seats in it which I used to polish to within an inch of their life and I kept the paintwork clean and fresh. I was also starting to build a relationship with Mam, dancing in the kitchen and joining in the sing-songs with her and I had the support of Siobhan and other friends to sustain me. The other thing I had discovered was the music of Bob Marley, which was life-changing.

He was introduced to me by Siobhan's sister Monica, who was married to an Italian, Franco. They were hip and cool and they seemed to have everything going on. Franco had been a DJ in England and he played this thing called reggae music that I had never heard before. As soon as he put a reggae record on the player, something took hold of me. I seemed to sense the beat and to dance to it instinctively. I started to listen to Bob Marley every day, loving the rhythm of the music but also the lyrics. The stories he told about black history, slavery and Rastafarianism were completely new to me and yet they felt familiar at the same time. I also identified with him because of his mixed heritage. His father had been White and his mother Black. As I listened and learned, I came up with a new story for myself. I was Jackie O'Brien, with a mother from Limerick and a Jamaican father. Whenever anyone would ask me about my identity, I would say, 'My mother is Irish, my father is Jamaican.' It felt like a comfortable jacket I could put on, that fitted well, and when people would insist, 'No, where are you *really* from,' I had just the answer. Like Bob Marley did with Rastafarianism, I did with reggae and with Marley himself: it resonated with me and it was a story I could completely identify with. Marley told me to be proud to be a Black person, that my roots were in Africa, like Marley's hero, Haile Selassie.

Now, not only did I have a new identity, but I also had a second family. I tended to collect families: my friends' mothers and fathers became my friends too. Mary, Siobhan's mother, had taken me under her wing, as had her sisters Monica and Patsey, and when Mary died, I was given the honour of carrying her ashes. I was considered one of the family. I think that I was embedding myself into other families because I was trying to get a sense of what family was like. If I didn't fully belong in my own family, perhaps I belonged in theirs, I reasoned. In that sense, I was something of a chameleon: I could be anyone I needed to be, depending on the person and the situation. The problem with that was when that was stripped away, who was I? The only person with whom I was truly myself was Siobhan.

Family and identity were two essential parts of my personal jigsaw. The third one was my sporting talent, which had taken a back seat to the other two, but which I knew I needed to take seriously if I was ever to play for my country. It was time to remember what Rita Spring had told me: 'God loves you as you are. Play for Ireland.'

Chapter 10

Finding Myself

I wanted to keep my promise to God, Mam, Dad and especially to the teacher who'd always believed in me, Miss Spring. It was time to put more effort into my chosen sport so that I could really give it my best. It had come really easily to me until now, so I hadn't taken it as seriously as I might. However, now soccer became my passion and my driving force. I used to dream about what it might be like to play for my country, to wear the green jersey and to be accepted by the place I loved. This shift in my identity and my growing confidence in my sport helped me to put the past couple of years behind me. I began to grow up and to branch out.

Joe Malone's pub in Denmark Street was the focus of the young Limerick scene at the time. It was a hangout for alternative people as well as a brilliant place to see live music. If you didn't drink in Joe Malone's, you missed out on an entire way of life. However, I also knew that I had to commit to soccer and so any spare moments were spent in the park or at the field at Hassett's Cross, in the shadow of Thomond Park. As I'd kick the ball and practise set pieces, I'd sometimes wonder what it might be like to play in its hallowed grounds, but then, I reasoned, there was no women's rugby so that was simply a pipe dream.

My hard work paid off. From the hospital, I moved to Krups Electronics in Limerick and played for their team, then I made the Limerick team. While we weren't the best team in the country, we held our own with some very close games. I was playing as a striker and I was a prolific goal scorer for the team. I was loving it: working hard in training and proving it on the pitch.

One day in 1980, after work, Mam handed me a letter. I was surprised: I didn't think I had ever received a letter addressed to me before! My heart almost stopped when I saw the logo of the LFAI, or Ladies' Football Association of Ireland. I was too excited to read the letter myself, so, with trembling hands, I passed it to Mam. She opened it and the smile on her face said it all. I was being invited to take part in national trials in Cork the following weekend. My dream was coming true.

I remember the look of pride on Dad's and my grandad Josie's faces. Dad told everyone who came into the shop and soon, it seemed as if the whole of Limerick knew my good news. When I walked through town, I'd get stopped and patted on the back. 'Best of luck, kid,' everyone would say. In that simple wish, I could feel the pride of my home town. *Finally*, I thought, *I belonged*.

Saturday couldn't come fast enough. Dad looked up the bus timetables to Cork and arranged for a friend of his to meet me from the bus and take me to the training grounds. With my boots polished and looking almost new, I got to the grounds, full of excitement and anticipation.

It was all quite intimidating. At 19, I knew very few of the other players, apart from a handful of girls I'd played against with Limerick, but my first thought was that they were at this game a lot longer than me. *What am I doing here?* I thought. This thought stayed with me as we got on the pitch to play, 11-a-side. As hard as I tried to shake off the feeling of not being good enough and to just play my natural game, I seemed to make mistake after mistake, bad pass after bad pass and to top it all off, I missed a sitter – an easy opportunity – on an open ball. I was devastated.

I knew at the end of the training session I hadn't made it, and even though the Ireland team manager thanked us all for coming and said he was impressed with the high standard, my heart was heavy. I knew I had let myself down. My natural shyness and nerves had got the better of me. On the bus ride home, I knew I'd blown it. I promised myself that if I got the chance again, I would make the team if it killed me. Whether or not that opportunity would ever come was anyone's guess.

Mam and Grandad did their best to cheer me up when I got home, but to no avail. I couldn't be consoled, not because I was disappointed, but because I knew it had been my own fault. Then Dad took me into the sitting room and sat me down. 'What happened at the training session?'

'My nerves got the better of me,' I admitted, head low. 'I didn't feel good enough compared to the other girls.'

'So, what are you going to do about it?'

I'd been ready for him to comfort me, to tell me it wasn't my fault, but instead, he'd asked just the right question. Instead of wallowing, I could take action. 'I'm not giving up on my dream,' I told him. 'I'm going to train harder and focus on my game.'

'That sounds like a plan,' he smiled, getting up to go.

'Do you know why the Irish team is so important to me?' I asked him as he opened the living-room door. He sat back down and I told him why. 'When I was in Birmingham, I was really homesick,' I explained. 'But it wasn't just for you all, it was for Ireland and Limerick and everyone at home. I also knew that because of the colour of my skin, some people would never accept me as Irish. But if I represent Ireland and wear the green jersey, no one can take my Irishness away from me.'

I could see by his eyes that Dad suddenly realised just how hard things had been for me growing up in Limerick. 'If that's what you want,' he said. 'Go and do it. I'll back you all the way.'

For the next few months, Dad came to my matches, shouting advice from the sideline and chatting to me about my game on the way home. I was more determined than ever to get on the Irish team, not just to make my family and Rita proud, but for myself, and to let the whole of Ireland know that there was no keeping this Black child of an industrial school down. That green jersey made me Irish and nobody could take it away from me.

I continued to train hard, and it was tough and often painful. Over the next few years, I played for Green Park, a team made up of like-minded players who were very determined to train and improve the women's game in Limerick. We had great success in our home town, winning both League and Cup on numerous occasions. I continued to be top scorer in the Limerick League, but I knew that I still had a lot to prove. The team manager was the same person who'd seen me at my original trials, where I'd let myself down, so I knew I'd have to work really hard to persuade him that I had what it took.

At the same time, my personal life was about to take a step forward.

It didn't start well, when I met Tom McCarthy in a bar one evening. I knew the family because they lived in nearby Ballynanty and I'd played with his six sisters growing up. His mother Susie ran the local pipe band and was known by everyone in Limerick. When I was about eight, she saw me one day and she said, 'You're the O'Brien girl, aren't you?'

I nodded politely.

She looked at me from head to toe, then said to one of the girls, 'Go and get one of the majorettes' uniforms, will you?' The girl ran off to the garden shed and returned with a lovely white silk dress, with green and orange embroidery on it. I thought I'd look amazing in it and could just see myself, marching up and down and twirling my baton. Then she held the dress up against me and said, 'This would be wonderful on you with the colour of your skin.' She wasn't really talking to me, but to her daughter. A plan was forming and her excitement was growing. 'Can you just see it? The O'Brien girl out in front of the band, with a big staff in her hand? We'd be the only band to have a Black lead in it,' she said. 'You'd look so exotic.'

My blood was boiling. I remember pushing the dress away. I said that it was way too short and that my mam and dad would never let me wear something like that. I walked out, leaving her with her mouth open. After a few seconds, she called after me, 'We could get some pants made for you instead?' I just kept on walking, banging the hall door behind me. Once again, my colour had been the only thing that someone had seen. The word 'exotic' was ringing in my head as I made my way home.

Now a full 11 years later, I wasn't prepared to like her son, Tom. Besides, I thought to myself, he liked my friend Phil, who played on the team with me. We'd been in Joe Malone's pub, jukebox blaring, Tina Turner and Milli Vanilli, and of course a bit of Bob Marley blasting in our ears, when I'd spotted Tom. He came over and sat down beside Phil and began chatting to her.

When I got up to go to the bar, he jumped up. 'Can I buy you a drink?'

'No thank you,' I said, my memory of his mother's band not forgotten. I went up to the bar then and bought my drink and thought nothing further about him. But then the following week he was there and the week after that. I presumed he was there to see Phil. If he was, though, why did he always offer to give me a lift home after the evening had ended? *Was he blind*, I wondered. Phil was mad about him.

His excuse was that I lived on his way home, which was true. Soon though, he was giving me lifts regularly. We'd chat about my soccer and his work as a vegetable wholesaler. He'd started his business with a horse and cart in Ballynanty and Kileely but had expanded into other areas. The horse and cart was soon replaced with a shiny new van and I got the impression he was a hard worker and well-liked by his customers, especially the women, who fell for his easy charm. But as we spent more time together, I began to find out more about him: that we shared a similar work ethic and had a lot of common interests: music, soccer, a love of poetry, in particular the poems of Robert Frost and Wordsworth, as well as a shared sense of humour. His mother might be a battleaxe, I thought, but maybe Tom McCarthy wasn't so bad.

One night, when he drove me home, he asked me if we could go for a walk. 'Why don't you show me around your old neighbourhood?'

I brought him to the handball alley, which was now a playground and we sat on the swings and told one another about our childhoods. I felt so comfortable in his company. Then I remembered his interest in Phil and asked him about it. He looked surprised. 'I'm not interested in any of your teammates,' he said.

That must mean he's interested in me, I thought. I wasn't sure what to make of it. 'Come on,' I said, 'There's one more place I want you to see.' I led him along the side of the local coalyard until we reached a large tree, beside which was a gap. We ducked down and climbed along a rocky area, which opened into a magnificent space. We sat on one of the rocks and looked up at the stars through the branches of the big tree. I told him my dreams of making the Irish team and he told me his, which was to build a house in the countryside, to get married to a nice girl and have loads of children, like his own family of 11. As I was only 19, I hadn't given much thought to the idea of having children, but Tom was 33 years of age. A gap of 14 years is a lot when you are young. It meant that we were in two different places in our lives, but I didn't see it clearly at the time.

When we walked the short distance back to my house and he said, 'Do you think you could be that nice girl?' I just smiled and went inside my house. The smile was still there as I quietly got into bed, not wanting to wake my sisters. Was I right in thinking that Tom McCarthy, son of Susie, was asking me to be his girlfriend? We were certainly a good match on paper. We both liked being outdoors: we'd go running in the forest in Woodcock Hill to build my stamina for my soccer, we'd fish for mackerel in Kilkee and would bring our catch home for Mam and Dad and the neighbours. Mam and Dad liked Tom a lot, because he was a hard worker, but also possibly because he was closer in age and outlook to them than to me, but I liked him too. A lot.

We'd been going out for about five months when he appeared on my doorstep, looking downcast. When I asked him in, he sat awkwardly on the sofa. Then he dropped the bombshell. 'Look, I'm going to Zimbabwe for a few months,' he said. I knew that his sister had married a Zimbabwean-Indian man some years before and had moved to the country. Tom explained that he'd be going to help out on a building project and I was completely taken aback. Zimbabwe was so far away. I didn't know if he was expecting me to ask him not to go, but I couldn't. I simply said, 'That's fantastic. It's a great opportunity and you should take it and enjoy every minute of it.' I meant it – but I also knew that I'd miss him.

Without Tom, I became more determined than ever to make the Irish team. I trained every single day, even though Tom was never far from my thoughts. He sent me letters every day, telling me what the country and its people were like, and he called at least once a week. He wrote the most beautiful poems to me, which I loved. Absence was truly making the heart grow fonder.

On a visit to my friend Siobhan's house one day, I got talking to her mother, Mary. 'How's Tom getting on in Zimbabwe?' she asked me.

'He loves it,' I told her. 'He writes letters every day and he calls me once a week to tell me all about it.'

Mary's eyes twinkled. 'That sounds like love to me!'

'Hmm. Mary, how do you know when you've found the right one?' I asked her. I knew from the tone of Tom's letters that he was serious about me and that when he got home, he might ask me to marry him.

Mary sighed. 'If Tom decided to live in Zimbabwe, would you be happy to give up your dream of playing for Ireland to go with him?'

My answer surprised even me. 'Yes,' I replied in a heartbeat. It was official. I was very much in love with this man.

Christmas 1981 came and went. Tom stayed in Zimbabwe and I felt lost without him. In February, I received a letter from Tom saying he could not stay away from me any longer. He asked me if I would be happy to see him on his return. 'Or has somebody else won your heart in my absence?'

I replied to his letter that day. 'I'm the kind of girl who can only give my heart to one person at a time. And my heart is taken by you.'

After four months away, Tom returned to Ireland. We became inseparable and before long, it was time to meet his mother, Susie. When he brought me to dinner in her house one Saturday, my stomach was turning somersaults. It had been years since I'd met her and I wasn't sure how we'd get on. I'd brought her a gift and gave it to her. 'Thank you, Jackie,' she said warmly. Then she told me about a bit of graffiti that had been written on the gable wall of their shop: 'Tom McCarthy's had a blackout. He's taking her out again tonight.' She then laughed heartily before asking me if I'd got the joke. I looked at Tom, who seemed not to be concerned or upset by his mother's enjoyment of this joke. I should have seen the red flag, but I was young and in love, so I just let it go, thinking I was being too sensitive. I wanted to get on with Susie, not cause trouble and so I said nothing.

A few weeks later, I was surprised when my mother called up the stairs to tell me that Tom was on the phone. I knew he was in Kilkee with his friend, Tony, fishing, and we'd arranged to meet when he got back, so I was surprised that he needed to call me.

'I've been on the beach,' he told me. 'And I found some white feathers, which reminded me of your beauty.'

This didn't make complete sense to me until he added that he wanted to ask my dad if he could marry me, to which I said, 'You'd want to ask me first.'

He laughed at this and said, 'I suppose I am asking you in a way. I want you to be the girl in my dreams. Please say yes.'

I did.

After that, everything happened so quickly. That night, Tom asked Dad for my hand in marriage. My family were delighted for both of us. As we both didn't want a long engagement, the wedding was set for 21 August 1982, some six months away. I would be a month shy of my 21st birthday.

Mam and I went shopping for wedding dresses but couldn't find one I liked. After all, I was a tomboy and wasn't used to climbing in and out of dresses, not to mention wedding dresses. We had arranged to go to Ennis to see if we could find something I liked, but one day, Mam came home from town with a big bag and a huge smile on her face. 'Come upstairs and try this on,' she said, so excited. In the bag was the most beautiful wedding dress, it fit like a glove when I tried it on. I loved it and gave Mam the biggest hug. 'Now, don't get mad at me,' she said, 'but you know how much I love a bargain. I was in my favourite charity shop and saw some wedding dresses in the back room and this one hit me.'

I just smiled at her and said, 'Sure, aren't I your daughter and I love a bargain too! It's perfect.' And it was. It wasn't a meringue, full of frills and flounces: it was sleek and fitted and simple. I wasn't one bit bothered that Mam had chosen it for me. Wearing a wedding dress wasn't top of my agenda and I was pleased that she'd done the hard work for me. Besides, I could wear a dress just for one day.

'Will you be wearing soccer shorts underneath it?' she joked and we both laughed.

I hesitated before asking the next question. In fact, I waited until Mam and I were heading to Birmingham to get my birth cert which I needed for legal reasons. It would be the ideal oppor-tunity, with her away from Limerick, to ask her more questions about my biological father. We were to stay with Auntie Marie but when I pressed Mam for answers, the result was the same: she got upset and refused to talk about it. When Mam wasn't there, one day, I quizzed Auntie Marie. And the secret began to grow legs. 'Your mother went to a Christmas party and was assaulted,' she said. 'Don't be upsetting her anymore because it's too painful for her. Be happy with what you have.'

In my head, here was the reason behind our difficult relationship. Was I the constant reminder to her of what had happened to her, I wondered. I couldn't blame her for not wanting to revisit the past. In that moment, I decided, I didn't need to know. I would leave it all behind me in Birmingham.

When I got back, the preparations were in full swing. Keane's Bakery had arranged to make the wedding cake free of charge to thank us for our custom over the years and we were to be the very last wedding held at the Parkway Hotel, before it was knocked down and replaced by a shopping centre. My sister Regina was to be my chief bridesmaid and my best friend Siobhan, my other bridesmaid. Everything was in place but with our families seeming to be more stressed by the planning than Tom and me, we longed to have an escape. Two weeks before the wedding a friend of ours came to the rescue offering us the loan of her flat in town while she was away. I was delighted to escape the mayhem for a bit, but I also knew that this would be the very first time that Tom and I would share a bed. I was pretty nervous and of course the Catholic guilt was never very far away. Here I was for the first time in my life, getting into bed with a man, even if he was soon to be my husband.

Somehow, it felt right with Tom. I loved him completely and we were starting our lives together. God would forgive us for not waiting the two weeks. Any thoughts I might have had about my feelings for other women were packed firmly away, along with the memories of darker times in my life. I was getting married now and it was time to move forward.

I was due my period on the day of my wedding but when the day dawned and it didn't appear, I was delighted. But there was a reason, which would come as a huge shock to me. On the day itself, I felt like Princess Diana at St Paul's Cathedral. Mam and Dad, my sisters and Gerard, were all looking fabulous in their wedding outfits and when the car arrived at the house, we all had a group hug. 'We'll miss you,' Regina said. 'There'll be no carol singing in the bed this Christmas,' she said sadly, referring to our yearly ritual.

'As soon as the house is built, we'll have carol singing in my place,' I reassured her. Tom had bought a site in Ardnacrusha, a few miles outside of town, and planned to install a mobile home on it for us to live in while his dream house was being built. I wasn't thrilled about starting life in a mobile home, but I knew it wouldn't be forever. Meanwhile, it seemed that half of Limerick had shown up on the street outside my childhood home to wish me well.

Just before we stepped outside, Dad paused and looked at me. 'Are you sure?'

I nodded.

'Are you happy?'

'I am. Now, let's go,' I said.

It must have taken us twenty minutes to get into the car and all along the way to the church, the road was lined with people waving at us. It felt like the Royal Wedding. I was princess for a day and Dad looked like the king of Ireland as he waved back at the well-wishers. When we arrived at the church, we had to make our way through the throngs of people at the entrance. I couldn't believe it. Were they there to see the most eligible bachelor in Limerick getting married to the luckiest girl in the world? Susie had reminded me many times that her son was a catch and that I was the lucky one. I, on the other hand, would never be good enough for him. Like Princess Diana, I was to find that there were three people in the marriage and one of them was very unhappy. That dynamic never changed.

Walking up the aisle on Dad's arm, all of this was ahead of me. Seeing the tears of pride and love in Mam's eyes, I felt that I was the luckiest girl in the world. Dad handed me over to Tom, who thanked him and turned to lift my veil, telling me that I looked so beautiful, he could hardly catch his breath. The ceremony was perfect, except when my grandad Josie roared with laughter when Tom knelt at the altar, revealing the price tag on the sole of his shoe.

After the family photos, we headed off for the wedding reception. Tom's sisters played the bagpipes, having learned in the pipe band and they played us into the dining area, which was a lovely surprise. The meal was lovely and the speeches were perfect. Then it was time for our first dance. I had picked the Lionel Richie and Diana Ross song, 'My Endless Love' but before Tom and I took to the dance floor, somebody tapped him on the shoulder. He turned around to face my old friend Christy. I couldn't believe it: Christy had been my very first boyfriend, coming to my rescue when I'd been so down and confused as a teenager. For a while, the two of us had been inseparable and even now, every time I bumped into him, we'd always talk.

'Congratulations,' he said to Tom, shaking his hand. 'Look after her or you'll have to answer to me.' We all laughed then Christy said, 'Is it okay if I have a dance with Jackie?'

'Of course,' Tom said politely. As I took to the floor with Christy, I could see the worried look on my mother's face, but she didn't have anything to worry about. Christy was the perfect gentleman, as he always had been. As the song ended he said, 'Look after yourself, Jackie. If you need anything, just let me know.' He placed a kiss on my cheek and walked away saying, 'I'll see you, kid.'

The night was a great success and everyone seemed to have a wonderful time. I was on top of the world. I had made the right choice with Tom, I thought. He might have been older than me by more than a few years but I felt that he was the one. He was so thoughtful and considerate too. When he heard that it was the joint birthday of two of my old teammates on Junior Keane's soccer team, he sent his brother William out to a jewellers to buy them each a gift. I can still remember one of them, Marion, thanking him. 'Who would ever have imagined that one day you would end up marrying the girl you forgot to pick up for the trip to Drogheda?' she laughed.

I looked at Tom, bewildered. '*You* were supposed to pick me up?' I was taken back to childhood, remembering my tears as I'd sat on the front doorstep, waiting for my lift to the tournament. A lift that never came.

Tom looked at his feet, guilty and sad. I leaned into him, smiled and said, 'Whatever you do, don't tell my dad it was you. We've just got married and I'm not ready to be a widow yet.' It was a joke, of course, but I could still remember Dad's words: 'If they don't think enough of you to pick you up, then you don't need them. Remember you're not above anyone but you're not below either. Keep your eyes level and we'll find you another team.'

'Keep your eyes level.' Dad's words rang in my ears as Tom kissed me and we headed for the dance floor again.

CHAPTER 11

A FRESH START

Three days before my wedding to Tom, I had been skateboarding around Kileely, with the wind in my hair. Three days after the wedding, I was in a mobile home in Ardnacrusha, on the building site that was to be our new home. In terms of me saying goodbye to my old life, it made for a stark contrast, but I always knew that building a home and having a family were Tom's priorities. I'm not sure if I really thought about my own needs at this time, but I do remember thinking, this is what love is. I really had no idea, because I hadn't received it when I most needed it. Those crucial years from babyhood to five had been spent in an institution and no amount of effort by my parents could fill that hole inside me. Maybe Tom could.

We had planned to go to Zimbabwe on honeymoon to see Tom's sister but had decided that the money would be better spent on the home we were building together. Our honeymoon was a night in Killaloe, arranged by Tom's best man. It was a lovely gift, but no sooner had we arrived on our wedding night than we both passed out on the bed from a combination of exhaustion and excitement.

I woke up the following morning bright and early. There was no sign of Tom. I began to wonder if the previous day had been a dream, but then I saw my wedding dress laid carefully over a chair and remembered that it had all been real. I lay there for a bit, reliving the whole event in my head: the way Tom had looked at me as we'd had our first dance together as a married couple, the crowds that had gathered to see me leave the house for the church, my whole family gathering to wish us well.

A knock on the door startled me from my daydream. When I went to answer it, there was Tom, a tray of breakfast in one hand and a pot of tea in another.

'There you go,' he said, putting the tray down on the bed. 'Get this into you. And when you're finished, we'll go down to Ardnacrusha.'

'Now?' I exclaimed. I'd been hoping for at least a lie-in.

'The site is too soft for the big lorry that has the mobile home on it, so I've had to get a lighter one to carry it into place. We have to be on site at 11 o'clock to check it.'

Welcome to married life, I thought, chewing on a piece of toast. When I'd finished, I made Tom toss the bed because it was so neat. He laughed but I said, 'Sure aren't we newlyweds? We can't leave the bed tidy.' However, in spite of the businesslike start to our marriage, we left the hotel hand in hand. I was truly happy. This is love, I remember thinking as we climbed into the car and headed for Co Clare. This must be it.

Three weeks after my wedding, I went to the GP to take a pregnancy test. That period that hadn't turned up on my wedding day still hadn't appeared. I was so naïve, I put it all down to the excitement of the day but a test soon confirmed the truth. I was pregnant. I was in shock. *I'm only twenty-one*, I thought. *I have my whole life in front of me and now I'm going to be a mam.* Everybody around me was giddy with excitement, but I was unsure. I was far away from Mam and from my family in Kileely, living in a mobile home in the countryside, albeit a comfortable one, with two bedrooms, a full bathroom and a separate kitchen. Tom had built a walkway from the backdoor to the shed where he kept his supplies but most importantly, he'd built an extra big room on the side for our expanding family.

At first, I loved our little home, improvised though it was. It was warm thanks to the stove given to us by Joe Malone, no less, and I used to enjoy playing house. I can still remember my first effort with an apple tart. I spent ages on it, carefully peeling the cooking apples and slicing them onto the pastry that I'd also made myself. I even decorated the lid with some pastry leaves. I served it with freshly whipped cream and big mugs of tea. It was only when I'd served it to Tom and the JCB driver digging the foundations of our new home that I realised my mistake. Tom's cheeks puckered and he couldn't conceal the wince as he bit into the sour apples. I'd forgotten to add sugar! Neither one of them said a thing.

If I wasn't a natural housewife, I was still a good footballer, playing well into my pregnancy and training as hard as I could, while expecting a baby. I didn't show until quite late on because I had good stomach muscles, and I was determined that after the baby was born, I'd return to playing. I suppose most mums-to-be think that life will just go on with a baby in tow, but Tom was very supportive of my choice to continue and I knew he'd be a great dad, even if I sometimes wondered why progress on our dream home was so slow. It seemed to go in fits and starts, with builders disappearing for long periods of time, which puzzled me. If Tom had put aside enough money for the building, why was it not progressing a bit faster? These concerns soon faded into the background as my bump grew and I began to worry about the birth. The baby was lying in the breech position, feet first and as my due date neared, I realised that that wasn't going to change.

Nothing had prepared me for the two-day labour that followed, even with Mam at my side. As midwives and student nurses came in and out of the room, eager to see the unusual breech presentation, I sweated and winced and roared my way through labour. The pain was excruciating, but finally my six-pound daughter, Samantha, came into the world on 28 April 1983. She was gorgeous, with her soft skin, tousle of black hair and big brown eyes. I fell in love with her immediately and I wondered if that was the way Mam had felt about me when she'd first held me in her arms.

Because I was young and fit, I sprang back to life pretty quickly. Even so, I was placed in the caesarean ward for extra care, but where every other mam was nursing her scars, I was bouncing around and helping them fetch and carry. The nurses would give mums who'd had a caesarean a rest and give the baby the first feed, so I assumed it would be the same for me. When it came time to feed Samantha, the curtain was whipped back and the nurse came briskly in. 'Will you be feeding the baby yourself?' she asked me, pulling the curtains around my cubicle.

'Of course I will,' I said, surprised.

'Lovely,' she replied, reaching in to the bassinet where Samantha was sleeping and lifting her carefully out. She handed the little bundle to me and then lifted my nightie and began to pull at my bra straps. 'Hang on,' I said. 'What are you doing?'

'Well, you're going to have to get your boobs out to feed the baby.'

'Oh no, no,' I protested. 'I want to give her a bottle.'

She hesitated while glaring at me. 'You know, I'm surprised that a person of your origins would want to bottle feed her baby.' And she marched off, leaving me with my mouth open.

Mam was enraged when she heard about it. 'What did she want you to do? Sit under a bamboo tree?' I didn't really know what to think. I was so young, I hadn't given breast or bottle-feeding much thought. I hadn't really considered what being a mum would be like and how I'd bond with Samantha. Now, I sat on my bed with her in her bassinet beside me and the thought of it all was overwhelming. *What kind of a mother will I be?* I thought. *Will I be good enough for my daughter?*

In those days, new mums stayed in hospital for five or so days and the other women on the ward took me under their wing, giving me advice about winding, feeding and changing nappies. They also listened to me talk about the site in Ardnacrusha and our mobile home, all the plans I'd made for the future. We became like a family, supporting each other until it was time to go home on our own. When I left the ward, I was laden down with baby clothes, bottles and other equipment, donated by the other mums. I thought they were helping me because I was a young mother, but it turned out that they'd assumed I was a Traveller. They had taken the fact that because my surname was now McCarthy, that I lived in a mobile home and had a 'site' literally. In fact, as I left one of them asked me if there were many other people on the site with me. The penny dropped. We all laughed, but it's not really funny how quick people can be to put labels on you. My colour meant that I would breastfeed naturally, and my name and the mention of a mobile home meant that I was part of a separate tribe. I chose to see the funny side of it but humour quickly became another form of defence, another piece of the suit of armour I always wore with other people.

I loved being a mum, cooing and fussing over Samantha, loving her every gurgle, the shock of black hair that was so like my own. I was fiercely protective of Sam and carried her close to me at all times. It wasn't fashionable at the time, but I never put her in a buggy or dressed her in frilly clothes – instead I took her everywhere with me. I found myself becoming Sam's protector, just like my dad. Woe betide anyone who would do anything to my child.

I was also determined that I'd get back to soccer, something that Tom understood and supported. Two weeks after giving birth to Samantha, I was back in training. As is always the way with these things, me becoming a mam had coincided with a big leap in my vocation. After years of playing for local sides, the Irish national team came calling. Later that year, I got a call-up and this time, I made sure to play my best game. Before I knew it, I was selected for the team and got my very first cap in 1983. I was elated. I had finally reached my goal to don the green jersey and play for my country.

There was only one problem: when Samantha was 11 months old, I became pregnant again, this time with Robert. I love my children more than anything but I couldn't believe that it had happened again and that by the age of 23, I'd have two children and be trying to make my way in my chosen sport. I was so anxious not to drop out of the competition that I continued to train with my local team until I was four months pregnant, before reluctantly dropping out. Nowadays, elite athletes are much more tuned in to pregnancy and training than I would have been: it never even occurred to me to put off pregnancy until I was older. Having a family was important to Tom and I wanted to make him happy and I loved being a mum. Robert made his appearance on New Year's Eve 1984. New Year has always been a special time for the O'Brien family. Tom and I were so proud. We had our family, our boy and our girl. Life was complete. Besides, as I told him, I was never going through labour again!

I was now at home with two small children racing around a mobile home. It was stifling in the summer and freezing in the winter and the stove rattled every time there was a gust of wind. The flue turned in the wind and I had to climb a ladder, get up on the roof and turn it back again so the wind wouldn't blow down the chimney. I can remember once placing Robert's cot close to the stove to keep him warm and a gust of wind shot down the chimney, covering him with a fine layer of soot. That said it all about our temporary life. When Tom got back from work that night, I was livid. I had no idea when we might be moving into the house of our dreams. We were still nomads after three years of marriage and I began to feel uneasy. Why were our lives not moving forward as I'd hoped? I knew that Tom helped his mother out a lot in her little shop and he often visited her in the evenings but I felt that I needed his company too. I didn't want to have to fight Susie for his attention, but it hurt. I was also confused about where Tom's money was going. The business was doing very well and yet he never seemed to be making all that much money or spending it on the house. I couldn't work it out.

One night Tom's van was rear-ended and he ended up in hospital with whiplash. He rang me to ask me to bring in a couple of things to him in hospital. Hastily, I threw a few things into a bag and rummaged through his sock drawer to find clean socks and underwear. I came across his bank book, a plastic-covered notebook which recorded every lodgement and withdrawal made over the previous few years. Curiously, I opened it and scanned the entries and withdrawals, unable to believe my eyes. *How are there so many? What has he been spending all this money on?* How were there separate bills for energy use, bills that weren't ours? I knew that he wasn't spending cash on the house, because after three years it remained half-built; and he and I lived modestly. We didn't have the lifestyle that this money could buy. I shoved the notebook back underneath a pile of vests and eyes watering with shock and dismay, I got his hospital bag ready. My head was spinning. It was Tom's money, but still, who else was he supporting apart from his family?

I would discover the answer to that before too long: he was supporting his mother, all her bills and her household expenses. I wanted my marriage to work, I loved my husband. I believed in marriage as an institution and I had my parents' long marriage as an example. My father had once been a heavy drinker, but somehow, Mam and Dad had managed to stay together through it all. I knew they loved one another. And while I might have once had feelings for other women, I can honestly say that I'd put them

behind me, because I'd met the love of my life. To me, a partnership is about hard work, loving somebody, holding their hand,
supporting them through everything, good and bad. For Tom, his
view of marriage was different. I think he put it in a box, to be
taken out and looked at among all of his other responsibilities: his
mother, his business, the never-built house. His own parents had
separated, with his mother continuing to run the shop and his dad
living upstairs in a flat, so the role models he had for a long and
successful marriage were very different to mine.

As the years passed, the gap between us began to stretch ever
wider until it was unbridgeable.

Over the next ten years, I was to play soccer for my country
and meet lots of different people from all walks of life on my
trips to Dublin. I was developing as a person, broadening my
horizons and becoming myself. But Tom had done his growing
and by 1992, when I was 32, the age he'd been when we'd
married, he was 45 and in a very different place in his life. We
were two people with very different views on the same relationship. I adored this man and I adored that he allowed me to fulfil
my dream of playing for Ireland. He never once complained about
that, urging me to go ahead and pursue it. There was always
food on the table and the children were always cared for. But
while Tom preferred the simple life, I would come back to the
mobile after an outing and lay the table for dinner as I'd seen it
in some fancy hotel. 'My God,' he'd say. 'Would you stop it? You
know, I don't need all this fancy stuff.' I took it that he was
saying that he didn't want or need me.

Eventually, we sought counselling to save our marriage. As we
drove to the counsellor, my heart was heavy. I knew what I wanted

to say but how would I say it in front of Tom? We were brought into a comfortable room and we sat side by side on the sofa. The counsellor sat opposite us, waiting. I decided that I'd break the ice. 'I love Tom, but I need him to be a husband, not just a father or a son. I want us to live in a house, not a mobile home. But most of all, I need to know that I am more than just the mother of his children.'

What the counsellor said to me next didn't surprise me. 'Look, it's not my place to take sides. I'm here to give you the tools to come to a decision either to work it out or to part on the best possible terms.' He said he felt I had had a period of great self-growth in the last seven years, but unfortunately, Tom had stayed still. At this, Tom got up and walked out in a huff, not liking what he was hearing. I stayed to hear what else the counsellor had to say, that we had outgrown one another emotionally, and he doubted Tom would ever change in his mindset to meet my growth. The only way for us to work was for me to put up and shut up and be happy with my loss. I went home that night and looked at my two children as they slept. I couldn't be the one to break up their happiness. I'd stay and see how it went after another cold winter in the mobile with frozen pipes and a dodgy chimney, me getting up and down on the roof to fix it.

But I decided that I wasn't spending that Christmas in the mobile. After seven years, I was done. I asked Mam and Dad if I could spend the two weeks of the Christmas holidays in their house with the children. And of course, they said they would be delighted to have us. Tom wasn't happy with this arrangement. 'If you're going to your parents', he said, 'I'm staying in the mobile and having Christmas dinner in Susie's.' That really upset me, that he would choose to spend Christmas Day with his mother and not me and the children. I made excuses to my parents, saying that Tom would be there first thing on Christmas morning to see the children open their presents and would come back after dinner, to put them to bed and have a Christmas drink with them, but I could see they were a bit uncertain about the idea.

Christmas was always such a happy time in my house. Mam loved it and we loved it too, singing Christmas carols in bed and eating a huge turkey dinner. But even though Tom was true to his word and we both made that Christmas as happy a time as we could for the children, I was heartbroken and miserable. I think we both were. And when New Year's Eve came, with all the celebrations that went with it, I was struck all the more by the fact that I was alone.

New Year's Eve was always a big event at the O'Brien's. The doors of the shop would be thrown open and the locals welcomed in for a sing-song and a drink. Dad would set up a table laden with bottles given to him by suppliers: whiskey, stout, brandy – he no longer drank but he was happy for his customers to share in the bounty. Early on New Year's Eve, he would put crubeens or pigs' toes, onto boil and Mam would fry batches of jumbo sausages. At midnight the doors of the shop would be thrown open and people from all over Kileely would come to eat, drink and be merry. The children would be woken for midnight then we'd struggle to get them all back to bed. Robert was a New Year's Eve baby, so the excitement was doubled. Robert was convinced that the celebration was for him! But this New Year's Eve of 1987, uncertainty hung in the air. At two o'clock in the morning, Tom said goodnight and left us to go back home. I knew that he was waiting for me to tell him that I'd return, but I'd made up my mind that I wouldn't. I was not going back to the mobile home.

I had no idea where I'd go until one day a local man came into the shop and asked if anyone might be interested in buying his parents' house. He'd inherited it but had his own house and was eager for a quick sale. No better place to advertise it than the local shop.

Dad came into the sitting room, where Mam, my two sisters and I were sitting chatting, drinking tea and he told us about the house. 'Who'd be interested in that, do you think?'

'How much is it?' I said.

'Three thousand pounds.'

'I'll buy it,' I said.

Everyone turned to look at me, eyes wide. I hadn't breathed a word to Mam and Dad about our problems. In those days, we didn't confide in our parents in that way, and their attitude would have been that if you'd made your bed, you'd have to lie in it. Marriage was a private thing and you didn't share your problems with the world. So while Mam and Dad were very supportive of us as a family, they didn't see our issues. They loved Tom and saw a hardworking man providing for his children, trying his best to get a forever home built. This was true but there was another side to things: that I was financially dependent on him, that money was tight and that after seven years, the house of our dreams had not been built. Of course, I never told them about my struggles with my mother-in-law either. Susie and I still found it hard to get along. I found it hard to understand Tom's closeness to Susie and the fact that this came at such a cost to me and the children. Much later a counsellor would wonder if, in some way, Tom was a substitute husband for her. This might be true.

'Look,' I told them, 'Things aren't going well between me and Tom. I need to move out, so I'll buy the house.' I did the sums in my head. I had a thousand pounds saved in the Christmas club but where would I find the other two thousand? Then I had an idea. 'Dad, I have a thousand pounds in the bank. If you lend me two thousand pounds, I'll work in the shop for forty pounds a week and repay you by the end of the year.'

Dad was taken aback. This was the first he or any of my family learned of any marriage problems. He thought for a while before saying, 'All right Jackie, as long as Tom agrees to it, I'll lend you the money.'

'Dad,' I said, 'this isn't about Tom. It's about me and the kids living in a house, not a mobile home.'

With a nod of his head, Dad went back into the shop and I could hear him tell the man, 'I have a cash buyer for you.'

It was now up to me to tell Tom. When he came over the next day to collect us, I dropped the bombshell. 'I'm not going back to the mobile home,' I said. 'There's a house in Kileely and I'm going to buy it. Dad's helping me out.'

To say he wasn't best pleased would be an understatement. 'I'm not buying a house in Kileely: the mobile is perfect until our own house is built.'

'I'm not asking you to buy it, Tom. I'm telling you that I'm buying it.'

He was silent for a long time before blurting, 'Well, best of luck to you,' and he turned on his heel and left.

My heart was heaving. After seven years of marriage, had I just given it all up? Could I do this on my own with two young children? In that moment, I reminded myself of everything I had come through and all the things I'd achieved. Hadn't I survived the industrial school? Hadn't I overcome racism, hadn't I made my dream come true of getting on the Irish team? I was bringing up two amazing children and they deserved the best. If I had to do it on my own, so be it.

I picked up the keys the next day.

CHAPTER 12

PRINCESS FOR A DAY

It seems an irony now that with my need to be loved, with a heart that needed to be filled, I had married a man who would not be able to fill it. Tom seemed to be detached, living in his own head and the more I attempted to bond with him, the further away he drifted. In a way, he wasn't unlike many Irish men at the time, but I wasn't like many Irish women. Of course, I was desperate for love, but I feel that I wanted what every person wants in a marriage: love, companionship, sharing. There was never a question or doubt in my mind: Tom loved me. I knew that. He just couldn't love me in the way I wanted to be loved, because he had to share me with his mother. That's the truth.

I often thought of Princess Diana at this time. Like her, I'd been a princess, albeit only for a day, and like her, I was discovering that there were three of us in my marriage. In Tom's account of our marriage, he would often say how beautiful I was and how much he loved me, but that my sexuality was the thing that came between us. My feeling is that my sexuality was not at play in our marriage. Maybe he saw something that I couldn't yet see myself, but I knew that I loved him completely.

And our relationship wasn't over yet. I had moved into my own little house in Kileely with Samantha and Robert, but Tom would visit often. If I was heading up to Dublin for training or going out for the night he would babysit, as well as seeing them every second weekend, but without either of us realising, we began to slip into being a couple again. Seven years together was a hard habit to break and quite honestly, I liked it. I loved being a mam, but I felt lonely and I think so did Tom.

Maybe neither of us was fully ready to move on, because one night, I came home with a few drinks on me and we ended up in bed. And that's how I ended up getting pregnant with my third child. Imagine telling my parents that even though Tom and I were separated, we were now having a baby together. Relationships are complicated things but the pregnancy brought a new freshness to Tom and myself. He didn't mention the third person in our partnership once during the early days of my pregnancy. We went out together on dates and had a lovely time. It was like being newlyweds again, heading to Joe Malone's for the night (I drank Coke!) and eating a takeaway on the way back to my place. We'd dip our fingers into the hot chips and talk about getting back together. 'It's still early days,' I warned him, but he seemed sincere.

Then I went to Dublin for training – I was still playing at this stage – and when I came back to my house, there was the strangest smell in the air. Pledge furniture polish. And then I spotted the plastic flowers on the mantelpiece. *Oh no*, I thought with a sinking heart. *We're back to square one.*

Tom had started to do little things around the place for me, like putting in a shower, or a new set of presses and fixing things in the children's bedrooms, but now, Susie was coming into *my* house and tidying it up. I brushed my hand along the mantelpiece and knocked all of the horrible plastic flowers off, then I opened the windows to get rid of the smell of Mr Sheen. I was livid and when Susie called to the door to collect a coat she'd left behind during her tidy-up, I had it out with her. 'What have you been doing in my house?'

'It's not your house,' she responded sharply.

'Oh yes, it is,' I barked. 'I paid for it with my own money.'

'Well, what's yours is his, isn't it?'

'It doesn't work that way,' I said. I turned on my heel, went back into the house and picked up her coat. I returned to the front door and I tossed the coat into the driveway. 'Now, you go or I'll send you after your coat!' She scuttled off down the front path. I felt a stab of guilt as I closed the door behind me, but more than that I felt rage. I'd put up with the situation for seven years and with a baby due, I felt that I was stuck with it. But when Tom came to visit and gave me a lecture on respecting his mother, I decided that rather than get into another argument, I'd write him a letter. I wrote it all down: the way I felt about always coming second, about his detachment and lack of interest in making our relationship work. At this time, I had a lot of gay friends, even though I hadn't realised yet that I was gay; I played agony aunt to them, listening to their stories of heartbreak and happiness. I could hear myself when one of the girls would ask, 'I fancy so-and-so. What do I do? How do I approach her?' I'd nod along and urge them to take a chance on love. 'Hopefully, she feels the same way,' I'd say optimistically, knowing that my own relationship was in turmoil. I poured all of this and more into my letter. It would come back to haunt me.

Stacey was born on 23 July 1989. She was beautiful, like her brother and sister. I looked down at her and it was one of those moments when everything slots into place. *I can't bring them up in this marriage*, I thought, looking down at her little fingers and her long eyelashes. What would they learn? We didn't fight: there were no rows in the little house in Kileely, but there was definitely an atmosphere. Tom now slept on the couch. When the older children would come down for breakfast, they'd greet him with a 'Morning, Daddy.' And he'd return at the end of the day to read them a bedtime story, before settling back down on the sofa. We were really only sharing the space. He was a good father and I was a good mother, but we were not in it together.

At one point in my letter to Tom, I'd written, 'I'm watching my friends and some of them are gay and I feel that they have better relationships than we do.' Tom understood this to mean that I was gay myself and that this was why I wanted a separation. The row was explosive and became violent. Tom self-published his own account of our marriage, *Susie's Son*, and he agreed that during this row, he'd lashed out and hit me and blackened both my eyes so badly that they were literally slits. I wouldn't stop him seeing his children, but our marriage was over.

I sat him down to tell him, adding that he was welcome to see the kids on alternate weekends, that we'd work it out, but once more, he lost his temper. 'I will come to see my children whenever I want to. You can't stop me.'

I wanted to be safe in my own home, so the next day I proceeded into the courthouse to get a barring order. The case went to trial and Tom tried to bring up the letter I'd written to him. The judge said, 'Mr McCarthy, it seems like you have problems within the marriage. Would you not just stay away? Maybe go back to counselling and take the children every second weekend. I'm sure your wife will accommodate this.'

'I will,' I said. 'I won't stop him seeing the children. We can make it as amicable as possible.' At this point, Tom turned and said, 'I'm telling you now, nobody will make arrangements as to when I can see my children. I will see them when I want, where I want and how I want.' I don't know whether it was wounded pride or fear that his children might be taken from him, but he was enraged. This worked against him, because the judge got annoyed with him and said, 'Mr McCarthy, you leave me no alternative but to put a barring order in place. You will pick your children up every second weekend from Mrs McCarthy's mother's house. You will not go near Mrs McCarthy's home.'

That was it. I was on my own. I had no car, very little money and no job. My children and my soccer were all I had. *I can hardly expect someone to mind three of them*, I thought, wondering if this would put an end to my career. Thankfully, my friends and my manager at the time, Linda O'Gorman, came to the rescue. I'd bring the older two with me and get a babysitter for Stacey. Linda was fantastic, saying, 'Listen, I'll make sure they're fed and kicking the ball around: you go out on the pitch and concentrate on what you need to do.' Somehow, I managed and that's why Samantha and Robert became such brilliant soccer players. One of my proudest moments was watching Samantha play for Ireland: in fact, we were the first mother and daughter to represent our country. Robert was also a fantastically talented player, making his own way in football in Limerick.

Looking back now, I really don't know how I managed to do it all, getting the children to school, working in the shop and then in a pub cleaning toilets, getting dinner ready, helping with homework, washing, ironing, training two nights a week and playing a match on Sundays. But I persisted, because soccer was my saviour, always there when I most needed it. Soccer was where I belonged.

CHAPTER 13

KICKING FOR GOAL

*Jacqueline "Jackie" McCarthy – 29.9.61 – FW – 5' 10" –
68th-minute sub for C Scanlan in plucky 1-0 defeat by Sweden
at Frank Cooke Park, 7.6.92 – listed as a Limerick United
player. Pike Rovers player subbed in for T Leahy in 2-0 friendly
win over NI, 17.10.93, Sligo. Twice-capped Greenpark United
"strong centre forward" and mother of two in squad for Eng
friendly 29.3.87. Made squad for 8.12.91 Euro qualifier in
Spain after making costly trips along the N7 from Limerick to
training sessions in Dublin for 7 successive weekends. One of
2 Limerick United players (w I O'Hanlon) in the squad. Was
"ever-threatening up front" in Ireland's 1-0 defeat by Spain
at Dalyer 22.3.92. A player of colour (Ireland's first? After
C Hughton and P McGrath on the men's side). Brum-born to
Irish mam and Jamaican father she never met, moved back to
Limerick as a 6-month-old baby, found it hard being only black
kid due to bullying etc. Favourite teacher got her into football:
Rita Spring, in St Munchin's Girls School in Ballynanty. Later
known as McCarthy O'Brien in honour of her beloved step-dad
Mickey O'Brien (a noted all-Ireland winning handball player
with a grocery shop). In a 2019 Limerick Leader interview she*

recalled winning 13 caps for Ireland from 1983 to 94 with a debut against NI at Chimney Corner FC. Kept playing/training between having her three children "understanding husband, Tom" then retired from soccer aged 33yo. Then got into Rugby Union and played for Munster and won 13 caps for Ireland, including at the 1998 World Cup, where World Rugby billed her as "Jackie O'Brian". Was a second row. One of six uncapped players in Fran Rooney's 16-player squad for NI Euro qual in Belfast 30.8.86 (w Green Park Utd). Played well in the 1-0 win, "McCarthy, a strong, fast-moving 19-year-old, was causing some anxious moments to the Northern Ireland defence" – Ireland's Saturday Night report. Top-scorer at the pre-season Lancashire Trophy, August 1991, with Limerick. "Jackie O'Brien" mentioned as missing from the Analog team photo ahead of the "All-Ireland soccer final" (President's Cup?) v Suffragettes at the Mary Immaculate College grounds, 12.12.81. Featured for Analog in a 2-1 win over Bank of Ireland (Limerick) in the Limerick League division 1 final, August 1981: "the signing of Julie Horan and Jackie O'Brien midway in the season gave Analog the forward power they lacked". Jackie O'Brien was a St. Joseph's player on the Limerick 'A' team which beat Cork 2-0 at Garryowen, 20.9.80. Player-coach of the University of Limerick team containing G Cross and M Gallagher which won the FAI Intermediate Cup, beating Burke Rovers 3-1 at Pearse Stadium, Limerick, 10.9.95. Mam of Sam McCarthy. Was the top scorer in Limerick when part of the Ballynanty team stunned 1-0 by G Cross-inspired Caledonians FC in the area semi-final of the LFAI under 15 Cup, Bateman Park, July 1977. Jacqueline O'Brien was on the Limerick League team to play the League

of Ireland as early as 6.11.76. A member of Greenpark's 1989
Limerick League and Cup double-winning side. From Kileely.

That is my soccer and rugby career in a nutshell, but what the
entry in the Women's Football Archive doesn't show is everything
that happened behind the scenes. Despite the fantastic team spirit
and a brilliant manager in Linda, at this time the ladies' soccer
game run by the Ladies' Football Association of Ireland or LFAI,
was very much an also-ran to the men's. We paid for our own
transport and meals and our kit consisted of cast-offs from the
men's team. I'm not joking! And, unlike the men's team, we didn't
receive post-match meals or days out when we played abroad. We
were basically put together on a shoestring, but what we lacked in
professional structure, we more than made up for in enthusiasm
and team spirit.

To play for my country, I needed to find a full-time job. Mam
and Dad were retiring from the little corner shop that had been
part of the fabric of Kileely, and so I would no longer be able to
work there. At the same time, I had three children to support.
For the first time in my life, I had to sign on. It had always been
a point of pride for me that I'd paid my own way, just as Mam
and Dad had but now, I had to accept my circumstances and turn
up at the social welfare offices to claim my £42 a week. I had to
make it work for us as a family. After four or five months, I was
switched to lone-parents' allowance which was a little bit more
in terms of money, but it was still a struggle. Still, I owned my
little house and Dad had passed his car onto me as he no longer
needed it. After forty odd years of hard slog, he and Mam were
happy to get the bus in and out of town to walk around the

market chatting or meeting up with friends for a cup of tea and a bun.

To pay for the running of the car, I managed to get a job cleaning the toilets in one of the local pubs. I earned £30 cash in hand for three mornings a week. I didn't think about it: I just did what I needed to do, but one day, one of my teammates said to me, 'Can you imagine, you're on the Irish international team and you're cleaning toilets, so you can have the money to travel to Dublin? I can't see any of the lads doing that.' She had a point but then, none of the lads needed to do it.

It was tough but I wasn't my father's daughter for nothing. I was determined to make it work and with the introduction of a scheme to get people on benefits back to work, I managed to get onto a course in Moyross, coaching children in sport. It was right up my street and even better, we also ran summer camps, which my children could attend. Now, I had two part-time jobs and was able to save my lone-parents' allowance to buy a bigger house a little further out of town, in Meelick. A year after my marriage break-up and with my permanent separation in place, I was settled into a good routine: I had a steady home life with the children and Tom had calmed down enough to accept the situation and collect them at weekends. But I was lonely. My soccer team became my only company and even thought I might have wanted to go out or to socialise, I'd tell myself, who would want to date a woman with three children? I wasn't exactly a catch.

One night, after a big win with my team, Pike Rovers, I arranged for my sister to mind the children so I could return to the club-house to celebrate winning the league. I didn't have many nights out so I was excited to let my hair down, knowing I didn't have to rush home to put the children to bed.

After the speeches and the dance, a guy appeared at my table and we started chatting. I found myself laughing for what seemed like the first time in ages. It felt comfortable and safe. We chatted with ease for hours as my friends came and went from our table and it was only when the evening ended that I realised how long we had been talking. As we stood there, he leaned in, placed a kiss on my cheek and said 'Look, I've had a great time talking to you. I'd love to get to know you better. Can I have your number?'

I was taken aback and refused. 'If you want it, you'll find a way to get it.' I don't know whether it was my natural shyness or that I hadn't come to terms with the fact that I was now legally separated, but something in me felt that if I gave him my number, I would be cheating on my marriage. It was in that moment I realised it was time for me to close the door and move forward. On the cab ride home, I felt both happy and sad. I had met a lovely guy and I hoped he would get my number somehow, but there was that sad realisation that Tom was now well and truly my ex-husband. Many years later, I bumped into him again. 'I did get your number,' he told me, 'but I knew Tom was a lovely guy and that you were only a year out of your marriage so I thought you needed more time. I'm sorry I didn't call. You will always be the one that got away.'

As time passed, things seemed to get a little easier. I was still holding down my two jobs, but the soccer season was over and with it the trips up and down to Dublin for training sessions. I had always wanted to own a nice car and to take Mam for a drive in it, and so I bought my very first car: a Nissan Bluebird! It wasn't a BMW, but it was a start. I picked Mam up and we drove around Ballynanty with the music blaring and the wind in our hair. It felt great – after everything she'd done for me, here I was, chauffeuring her around. When I got back, Dad appeared to inspect the car and winked at me, as if to say, 'Well done.'

In 1992 after a match in Dalymount Park with the Irish team, Linda O'Gorman announced that instead of the usual soup and sandwiches eaten under one of the stands while watching the men's game, she was taking us all to a restaurant to celebrate. 'It's on me,' she added. We were surprised but delighted. After all, we'd won a historic match away against Spain, and we deserved it. We might not get the nice hotels or be greeted at the Irish Embassy in Madrid, but as Linda said, 'You work hard and make many sacrifices to play for your country. You shouldn't have to sit under a noisy stand and have a bowl of soup and a few crappy sandwiches.'

Just over a week later, her short time as our first woman manager was over. Apparently, the FAI had heard that she had paid for our celebratory meal herself and they found it disrespectful. They were happy to spend money but not on our success, it seemed. And after Linda had got our first win away in Spain, when we'd won 1-0.

I was upset to hear this, as she was a good player-manager: she seemed to bring out the best in us as a team, and she had created a safe and respectful environment, not only for me and the other players, but for my children. Thanks to Linda, I had the freedom to play. I'm forever grateful for that.

Mick Cooke was to be senior manager of the ladies team. I knew that Mick was experienced but not much more than that. When a new manager comes in, there's always something of an upheaval. He or she doesn't know you all that well and you have to prove your skills all over again and wonder if you'll fit in the new plans. So I was delighted when I got the call-up for trials for the new season. This meant that I was on Mick Cooke's radar and would hopefully make the panel of 25 or so players for the team. I was thrilled.

But the atmosphere at the training camp was very different. With Linda, it had been a real family atmosphere. She allowed us to be ourselves, both on and off the pitch and she was approachable and flexible. With Mick Cooke, the feeling I had was one of anxiety. He had a way of instructing that felt less flexible, less relaxed. We found that we had to follow instructions and do as we were told. The team felt like more of a boys' club than a women's soccer team. The belief that was put out there was that we were playing as Irish internationals now and wouldn't get handled with kid gloves. The men weren't, so neither should we. And we were to do as we were told. The language was more combative, less patient. I had the constant feeling that I was stupid and failing to understand what I was being asked to do, rather than being encouraged to develop my skills. Gone was the collegiate vibe that Linda had worked to develop.

There was no way I would bring the children into this setup. Thankfully, they were old enough now to be looked after by Mam and Dad, which was handy, because I just didn't feel comfortable bringing them up to this new regime. I'm not sure if I was the only woman with children on the team, but Linda understood that my children weren't a barrier to my playing for my country. I had the feeling that the new manager might not see things in the same way, that I might be told that the training camps weren't a kindergarten.

Soccer is a team sport, and if it works well, the team becomes like family. But if the leader of that team can't be approached with certain problems, that can have a knock-on effect on your sport. I had no problem saying to Linda that my marriage was on the rocks at the time. She simply said, 'What can I do to help you to make sure that you stay on the Irish team?' I didn't feel that I would be able to say that with this manager.

A good coach will always take every facet of you, not just your skill on the pitch. Your skill on the pitch will be affected by your mindset off the pitch. When Gareth Southgate was managing England, I always thought he had that paternal vibe about him, that the players genuinely seemed to like him.

In my first match playing under Mick Cooke's management, I was a substitute for the first time. I was disappointed, but because it was a new manager in a new system, I thought I'd simply work harder in my position of centre forward and find my way back into the first 11. I told myself that even if I came on as a sub, I was still part of the team. I was good with that. I went home, worked harder, trained harder, looked at what he wanted, and I started to bring that into my local soccer so that I could hone my skills around what the team needed. But to my surprise, I was dropped completely from the squad – and my replacement hadn't even made the first team before. She hadn't even been a sub. It's easy to sound bitter, but I felt the injustice of it. I thought, *well, that's it.*

The Irish women's soccer team had been withdrawn from professional competitions because it was felt we weren't strong enough to be competing after being hammered by Sweden 0-6. It's true that when you get a beating like that, it can be very detrimental to your mindset. Mick Cooke had been in charge for about a year at this stage and perhaps he didn't want us to lose confidence completely. We could play international friendlies and focus on our skills and on improving as a team. They were still internationals. You were still representing your country.

Then the comments came, the locker-room banter that wasn't really banter. The gay players were at the receiving end of so-called jokes that a good man was all we needed to sort us out. It was insidious, always there, a creeping sense that everything wasn't right, that boundaries were being crossed and player safety was not respected, but at the time, it was hard to pin down.

We were all desperate to be on the team, and none more than me. For me, playing for Ireland was the most important thing. My need, as a Black person, to be visibly Irish overrode any discomfort that I might have felt in the squad. I wasn't going to walk away, no matter what. None of us were and the coaching/ management team knew that. We didn't have the status of the men or the money but in all other respects, we felt like professionals, because we took the game seriously. We paid our own way. We never asked for anything. We just wanted to be allowed to play for our country.

It was really after the heartache of being dropped for the squad that my determination grew to get back in there, to shut up and get on with things, to train harder and better. If being off the team could feel this bad, then I would get back on the team. My chance came in a friendly against Northern Ireland in Sligo. I was really excited about it, because I was picked as a substitute – I was back on the squad. A friend of mine, also from Limerick, was playing so we had a huge entourage of supporters there to watch us. About twenty minutes from the end, the manager beckoned me to go on. So, off came the tracksuit and I ran onto the pitch in my green jersey. I was back and I was going to play my heart out and keep myself in this squad.

We won the match 2-0 and everyone was in high spirits. We returned to our hotel, had a meal and celebrated with a couple of pints in the lobby. Mick Cooke was passing through the lobby and spotted me. He beckoned me over and said, 'Come up to my room in five minutes. I want to have a chat with you.'

Here goes, I thought. I ran potential scenarios through my head. *Maybe*, I thought, *he's going to tell me*, 'Look, you're doing well. You've got to work on X, Y and Z, you know.' It was unusual to be called to a manager's room. All the talking would normally be done in training or a meeting room where the coaches would be present and the assistant manager, but I ignored my gut feeling. At this point, rumours were swirling about inappropriate behaviour with some of the players. There was even a rumour that the manager might be sleeping with one of the players, but they were just rumours. We might have our suspicions, but there was a sense that nobody was to be trusted. I didn't know who I could talk to and who I couldn't. Looking back, of course things weren't right, but in the early 1990s, we were in the Dark Ages.

Still, something in me said, 'Make sure somebody comes and gets you out of there within five minutes.' I approached one of the girls and said, 'Listen, can you do me a favour? I'm going up to the room for a chat with the manager. Come up and knock on the door after five minutes and say I'm wanted downstairs.' Her eyes widened but she nodded.

In the room, the TV was on, tuned to a soccer match. Mick Cooke was reclining on the bed, head against the headboard. He put his hand on the mattress and said, 'Sit down.' I looked at the chair in the room and hesitated before perching on the edge of the mattress. We talked a little bit about the match and then about my game. 'How did you feel you played?' he asked.

'I thought I had a good game but I know I can do a lot better. I'm getting used to the style of play you want. I'm working on it,' I said politely.

'Yeah, and you've done well.'

I sighed with relief. I had expected a talk along the lines of 'You're not fitting into my plans,' and this was unexpected. I waited to see when he'd say, 'okay, off you go.' I was shocked when he turned his body towards mine and pinned my shoulders back, leaning in to kiss me. Surely, he knew that I was one of the gay players on the team? This wasn't just about power and lust, I realised, but about denying who I was as a human being. I was frozen, unable to move. Then I heard my friend's voice in the corridor, a loud banging on every door (she'd forgotten his room number) and it woke me up. I literally rolled off the bed and said, 'I've got to go. My friend's looking for me.' I ran from the room.

In 2024 I took part in a documentary on RTE television, *The Girls in Green*, when the full extent of what was going on at this time in the Irish women's team was revealed. It turned out that what I'd experienced had happened to other players. I wasn't alone, but in that atmosphere of distrust and isolation, I'd thought I was. That was part of the plan, I realise now. It felt like a lose-lose situation. I can remember thinking, *if you kick him, there goes your career. If you respond or allow it, there goes your sanity and your sense of wellbeing. How much do you want that green jersey?* I had a sense of impending doom. If I got back on the Irish team, would he try it again? If I didn't accept his advances, would I get a letter to say that I was dropped? All these questions were swirling around my head.

A week or two later, I had my answer. My friend called me to ask me if I was planning to stay with her for the training session.

'What training session?' I hadn't even received a letter.

The last time I saw Mick Cooke was when I walked out of that hotel room in Sligo. It would be the last time I ever played for the Irish women's soccer team. My dream was in tatters. That man had taken so much more than he could ever know. People would say to me and I would say to myself, 'sure, it was only a kiss.' It was momentary, his hands on my shoulders before I'd heard my friend and made my excuses, but I knew that wasn't the truth. Other players suffered too. Olivia O'Toole, who went on to be the country's most capped woman player with 130 caps and 54 goals, was dropped from the team. Coincidence maybe, but she was a truly amazing player who'd be first on any team sheet. After Mick Cooke's departure, Olivia returned to the team and got another 20 or so caps and scored many more goals for her country. We were told that she wasn't turning up for training, that the reason she was dropped was because of her playing, but her tally of goals after his departure disproved that.

In my case, I would go on to play rugby for another seven years, making internationals, going to European championships, captaining the team. So it wasn't my ability as a player or my fitness or anything else like that. Mick Cooke had been a big fan of bleep tests, where you run increasingly quickly to test your aerobic fitness and I'd excelled at those. I was 32, but I was super fit. I was still scoring goals for my county and my club. I was on the first 11 with Limerick. I was on the first 11 with Munster. But not the Irish soccer team.

We all understand that we can get dropped from a team for any number of reasons, but there's a process. The manager will discuss your performance with you, invite you to improve, encourage you to keep trying. But *The Girls in Green* proved that players were dropped for other reasons, reasons that didn't make sense.

For me, I had the sense that in taking that green jersey away from me, my identity was being taken away at the same time.

We all have to face the day when we start to slow down, when we're not good enough, or fit enough. I'd be the first one to put up my hand when that happened, but I knew that at 32, I still had much more to give. I continued playing for Limerick and for my local team but without a larger goal to aim for, I started to lose my love for the game. I stopped watching the men's game on TV and even though I was still training, I stopped going to see other women's matches. My enthusiasm for soccer was only rekindled on the 50th anniversary of the women's game in 2024, when I began to get invited to events and meet up with old friends.

That feeling of what we'd achieved in spite of everything came out, a renewed sense of pride.

I went to my first Irish women's international in October 2024 to celebrate the women's team going to the World Cup and it was a brilliant occasion. At the same time, I knew that the documentary was going to be released, telling a much darker story about women's football. It was held back until the Irish women's team had gone off to the World Cup, so that they wouldn't be at the centre of a big media storm, but it still made a huge impact. It was hard to watch, but my story and that of what happened to so many of the younger girls was finally out for all to see. The drinking, the inappropriate behaviour, it was all there in the documentary. Of course, it's up to others to tell their stories, but what I found interesting was the fact that we all thought it had only happened to us. That we alone had been singled out for attention and exploitation. We stayed quiet because if we didn't, it would look as if we were just complaining about not being selected for the squad. If we'd spoken to each other, the pattern, the truth would have emerged. Some women became alcoholics, others tried to commit suicide, all because of the hold that Mick Cooke and a coach on the junior team had over them. It was seen as the price we had to pay to keep our place on the national team. Far too high a price.

CHAPTER 14

FIONA

So, here I was, a young woman, a separated mother of three, working two jobs to make ends meet and facing the end of my international soccer career. I had spent so many years with one goal in mind and I'd fought so hard to make it happen that now, I couldn't see what lay ahead of me. I had no idea where I might go next, as a sports person, but also as a woman.

Then into my life came Fiona. We bonded through our love of sport and what we also had in common was that we were both gay, and both of us were figuring out exactly what that meant.

We played locally together and one evening after training, we got talking. 'How do you know?' she asked me.

I knew what she meant. It wasn't just a single moment when a lightbulb went off in my head. It was more like a gradual awakening, a sense that relationships with other women were right for me. What I had cut off from my life as a teenager was coming back to me now as an adult. 'Well, to be honest with you,' I told her. 'I'm relatively new to the gay scene,' and I explained to her that I'd had a brief relationship that I'd given up pretty quickly because of my fear that if I was open about it, the court might take my children from me. It was the 90s and Ireland was still very much in the dark about gay relationships.

We talked for a long time and we ended by making a pact that we'd always be there for each other while we were navigating this new world. How would we come out and to whom? How would we deal with a woman coming into our lives? We discussed all of this and more and what had started off with a conversation led to us spending more and more time together. Initially, we were just chatting but one night, the kiss happened. Suddenly, we both wondered, could this be us? Could we actually be right for each other? We were both coming to terms with our sexuality, so we were on the same page and we were very upfront in talking about it, so it felt very natural. Still, I was conflicted. I'd got over the fear of my children being taken from me, because I knew that I was a good mother, but I sometimes found myself wondering if my next relationship would be with a woman or a man. By the same token, I had more and more visibly gay women as role models so that gave me the strength and the courage to be myself and to say to myself that if the next person was a woman, I'd embrace it. There were so many conflicting emotions: my children didn't know that I was gay at this stage because I hadn't been openly affectionate with the previous woman but with Fiona, it would be hard to hide.

Fiona had to go away to the USA for a couple of months, which gave us both time to think. While she was away, I realised that I missed her so much. When she came back, I knew that I'd fallen for her. We both wanted to see where things would go. But first, I needed to tell the children. They'd met Fiona a couple of times but she was still 'a friend' in their minds.

The children had been around gay couples without it ever having been said. They just knew that the couple came as a pair, without knowing the term 'lesbian' or 'homosexual', but I knew that I needed to be more direct. I sat them down and said 'Look, you know that I loved your dad . . .'

They all nodded.

'But take Mary and Teresa on the soccer team, they love one another. And they're together as a couple in the same way as your dad and I would have been.'

Again, the nods, and one of them said, 'Yeah Mam, we know.'

'Well, that's the way I feel about Fiona.' I told them that Fiona and I had feelings for one another and we loved one another and we were going to see where our relationship could go.

There was a lot of shrugging and very little surprise. The kids were fine with it because they absolutely adored Fiona. My younger daughter Stacey, used to go with Fiona to her parents' house for the weekend, because she loved staying there and being spoiled. Fiona was already part of the family and us being together seemed natural.

Fiona showed me unconditional love. I felt really, really loved by this woman and I knew that she always had my back. She put me to the front of her thoughts in her plans and I hadn't experienced that in my marriage. Here was somebody prioritising me in the way that I prioritised her and it felt fantastic. And when we announced our relationship to our friends, they were so happy for us. People thought we were good together and we were: I loved her and she loved me. We were so happy together.

The only thing was that Fiona was very closeted. Apart from my family and our teammates, she hadn't told anyone that she was gay, either in her work or in any other area. Crucially, she hadn't told her parents. During our three years together, she moved in with me but her family thought that she was living with a friend in a sort of house share. I knew that her mam and dad were a lot older than mine, but my mam and dad adored her. I didn't hide her, but nor was there any big announcement that Fiona and I were together. She just started coming around more and more and being included in family events, but while I was openly gay, Fiona hid her sexuality from the outside world.

Initially, it didn't seem to matter, because Fiona was such a huge support to me. She helped me through so much and she offered me so much that it seemed like a small price to pay for the secrecy in our relationship.

One day, I happened to be at home when a documentary appeared on the television. It was called *Dear Daughter* and in it, a woman who looked a bit like me, was telling her story. Her name was Christine Buckley. She was the child of an Irish mother and a Nigerian father and had been sent to the notorious Goldenbridge School in Inchicore at the age of four. She had been dressed up in a little red coat and told by her foster carer that she was going to visit Santa, but instead, the gates of the industrial school opened then closed behind her. What she described next was a world of hell, with regular beatings, presents given then taken away, being forced to make sets of rosary beads until her fingers bled. I watched in a trance. Why was this woman telling my story, I wondered. Why had she been dressed up every Saturday to see visitors just like me? Why didn't she know that her visitors were her parents? When I looked at her, I saw myself.

The next thing, I was in the bathroom, sitting on the floor beside the toilet, bawling. Fiona heard me and came running in. 'Jackie, what's wrong?' I broke down and I cried for a full hour in her arms repeating, 'I want my mam. I want my mam. I want my mam.' What I was crying for were those five-and-a-half years lost to me and my family. In Fiona's arms, I was baby Jackie and I wanted my mother. The mother I hadn't had when I was a baby. But I knew that I couldn't have my mother in the way that I needed, because she didn't know what it would have been like to hold one-year-old Jackie, two-year-old Jackie; I was five when I got out of the Mount. And then, she hadn't been able to hold me because it took me two years to begin to trust her and my new family. By then it was too late: I was too tall to be held in my mother's arms.

The loss of it hit me with such force that it felt like a physical blow to the chest. All I could do was sob my heart out and call repeatedly for my mother, while Fiona sat with me and held me. 'Jackie, you are cared for. You are wanted. You are loved by me and by your mother and by your children.

It was overwhelming. All my life, I'd worn a suit of armour: if I was loved or wasn't loved, I could take it. It didn't matter to me. But in that moment, there was a chink in the armour. Little Jackie was coming out to say, 'Please hold me. Please love me. Please want me.' And Fiona was there. I had found unconditional love. In that moment I promised myself that nothing would ever stop me from feeling the love that I had right there and then from Fiona.

And I did feel it. Fiona had given me just what I needed and had been there when I needed her most. I'll never forget that.

But there was also that unresolved issue in our relationship, which would emerge every now and then. One day, I said to her 'What'll it be like when you tell your parents? How do you think they'll react?'

'I'll never tell them,' she replied simply.

Oh, I was blindsided. How could I see the rest of my life with Fiona if she wasn't being fully honest about our relationship, I thought. I knew that she loved me – she'd shown me that – and I knew that this was about her, not me, but I had the creeping sense that I wasn't enough for her. If I had been, surely, she would have told her parents about me. I wasn't able to articulate it at the time, but deep down, I knew what I was feeling. I'd always be a secret. My name would always be associated with shame. I'd had too much of both as a child and I couldn't live with secrets now.

Suddenly, the life I had been able to see stretching in front of us had vanished. Later, if I was asked, I would say to close friends that if I won the lottery in the morning, I would have given it up to go back to the way I felt about Fiona. But I couldn't go back. We ended the relationship with heartbreak on both sides. It was hard to leave a relationship that had been so loving and caring behind. Everything about Fiona was amazing: her love for me, her support, her fondness for the children but there was that one thing. Maybe it sounds egotistical but if you can't be honest about who you are, that's pretty insurmountable as obstacles go.

To this day, though, we're still friends. There's nothing wrong with her choice, it's just that I know I couldn't live like that. That's why Pride and other gay events are so important for those who are out and those who aren't. It's a safe zone to be able to hold your partner, to be able to dance with your partner in public, to be true to who you are.

The funny thing is, Fiona was still living in my house when I met the woman with whom I would live for the next 18 years. Fiona needed time to work out her next steps and I was in no hurry for her to leave, so just like the Paul Brady song, we did the long goodbye. We moved into separate bedrooms and while I cried in my bed at night, I could hear her crying in the bedroom next door. But I knew that there was no going back.

CHAPTER 15

LEARNING A NEW CODE

With my soccer career over, I found a new confidence in coaching, finding that I had a talent for the fitness side of things. I loved coaching the UL soccer team, taking them on runs up the steep incline of Woodcock Hill all the way up to the radar station. We'd look down over the city and I'd see the magnificent Thomond Park in the distance. I'd always told myself that one day, I'd play there. As a soccer player, it was a pipe dream, I knew, but what was the harm in dreaming?

By the end of our training sessions, the girls and I were super fit. I was a natural athlete, tall at 5' 10", and even though I was a scrawny thing, I was strong. It must have been all the bags of potatoes and briquettes I'd carried over the years! With UL, we won the league and a football season, so I was delighted with the success. Maybe I'd found my niche in coaching and fitness, I thought.

I knew that some of the girls switched codes to play rugby during the winter, but I'd never even considered it. I was too old, I thought, and I had no idea of the rules of the game, beyond watching my heroes, Munster. Besides, the women's game was new at this stage, having only started a couple of years before.

Then one of the girls asked me if I'd be interested in coming out to Old Crescent Rugby Club to help them with their fitness. One door closed and another door opened, and before I knew it, that dream of playing in Thomond Park had become a little bit more real.

It wasn't promising to begin with. Old Crescent already had a fitness coach, so that was that, I thought sadly, preparing to pack my stuff up and head home. Next thing, a rugby ball was thrown at me. 'Come on!' the coach yelled. 'Fall in!' I might as well, I thought. It might be a bit of fun. I stumbled around the pitch, fairly clueless, until it came to the line-out and the coach said to me, 'Get in there, you're in the line-out.'

I had to turn to one of the girls and say, 'Where do I stand and what happens?'

'We'll lift you and you jump up and catch the ball – okay?' she replied.

Thanks to my height and weight that was easy, so when the moment came, I caught that ball and passed it and the feeling was like a bolt of lightning going through me. *This game is absolutely brilliant*, I thought.

After the session, the team manager took me aside and he said, 'Right, have you signed your forms?'

'I actually came out to coach the team . . .' I began before he interrupted. 'I'm the coach, but here are the forms. You're signing as a player: you're some jumper.'

By the end of the night I was signed and the following Sunday, I played my first match. What a baptism of fire! We were playing Blackrock Rugby Club, from Dublin, and we were totally out-classed. I can still remember standing upright as this woman ran towards me thinking, I'm going to stop her, but she hit me with the force of a speeding train. I'd say she pushed one of my shoulders 180 degrees until it met the other. But it didn't put me off – I thought, *this game is for me and I'm going to take it seriously.*

It brought back such happy memories, of dancing with my friends in Shannon Rugby Club and slipping over the walls of Thomond Park to watch Munster beat the All Blacks. I loved the genuine family atmosphere and the camaraderie, which was different to that in soccer, so I made it my business to learn the rules. I played as a loosehead lock, number four, in the second row of the scrum and because of my jumping skills, I excelled in the line-outs. I also became very good at tackling and my soccer training helped me with the ball. Within six months, I was putting on the jersey for Munster. I couldn't believe it and the dream I'd always had to play for my country came alive again. If I could make the Munster team, maybe I could also make the Irish team. I could get back the green jersey that mattered to me so much.

I trained and I trained and that year, we managed to beat the mighty Blackrock. It gave us huge satisfaction, because we were a raggle-taggle collection of soccer and rugby players, all new to the game, whereas the Blackrock women had practically been playing since birth. It was tougher to play my old friends in Shannon Rugby Club, but I was there to play, so I got on with it. One of the girls on our team used to make a muscle rub for us out of a mixture of poitín and wintergreen, which worked really well, but in rucks, the smell was potent. The Shannon team would say that we'd all been drinking the night before!

We had two great seasons, before the excitement fizzled out a little, with some women returning to soccer, but it was at this stage, in 1994, that I was approached by the manager of the Irish women's team, Des Byrne. He came up to me after a Munster tournament and said 'You're good at this. How long have you been playing?'

'Just coming on for a year,' I said. His eyes widened. 'I can imagine what you'll be like in two years' time.' And then he said the magic words, 'Would you like to play for Ireland?'

'I'd love to play for Ireland,' I said. Little did he know just how much I longed to play for my country. 'Right,' he said, 'I have to tell you it'll cost you about four-and-a-half grand because we're going to the European Championship next year.'

I misheard him, thinking he was giving me four-and-a-half grand and I thought, *wow, I've landed on my feet here: they're going to pay all my expenses.*

'That's brilliant!' I said.

'No,' he said. 'I don't think you heard me correctly. That's what it's going to cost you in loss of earnings. You're going to have to come to Dublin for training sessions, you're going to have to buy your gear and pay for your travel expenses. With everything else, it'll cost about four-and-a-half grand.' Seeing my expression of shock, he added, 'I'm sorry to put you on the spot but I need an answer because if you're not going to be my player, I've got to approach somebody else, but you're my number one choice.'

I was back to square one, starting a new code with the same issues: no money, no kit, nothing, but Des had told me that I was his number one choice, so I'd find the money somewhere. Thanks to Old Crescent, I got a job in a bar to pay for my expenses which really helped. At this point, we were playing in an All-Ireland league, which meant trips to Belfast, as well as Dublin and Cork – all over the country. Thankfully, because of the family atmosphere, my children were able to come with me to some matches and to training. At home games, we all pulled together and everyone in the clubhouse would pitch in to make sure the kids were fed and watered and looked after – and given a rugby ball to go out and play. Also, one of my teammates, Grainne Cross, was a great help to me. The Crosses are steeped in rugby and her mother would often babysit for me while I played.

After the chilly winds of soccer, this was a lovely warm breeze. There was no judgement of the fact that I was a woman with children or that I was gay. There wasn't even a whiff of homophobia: instead there was a feeling that we were really supported. I had truly landed on my feet. *How did this happen to me*, I wondered. *How did I get so lucky?* It was hard work, of course, but the IRFU did everything to help me. I had the bar job and then I joined a rugby-coaching scheme in schools, which was fantastic. Most of the kids were passionate about hurling, Gaelic football and soccer, so it was great to go into the schools in Limerick and get them interested in rugby. In fact, one of my players was a very young Keith Earls: his dad had grown up in Kileely, so I knew the family and while I can't claim the credit for his career, I like to think that our few coaching sessions helped set him on his path.

Limerick has produced some amazing rugby players from across the social classes. It's less of a middle-class game than in Dublin. On the rugby pitch, we used to joke that you have the cream puffs and the donkeys. The cream puffs are the pretty guys out the back and the donkeys are the pack. In a way, Limerick were the donkeys and Dublin were the cream puffs! In Limerick, rugby came from the Welsh dockers who worked at the port and it came up the Shannon, so it started off in the city with working-class roots. By the time it reached Dublin, it became much more middle-class. We had that divide for years: that Dublin were more skilled – the brains of the operation – and Limerick provided the brawn. At club level, it was often very tribal but at the national level, we all came together and played as a team.

However, even at club level, it didn't matter really where you came from. It was your talent that mattered. I made some great friends through the game in Leinster rugby and even in Blackrock. They appreciated my ability. I also loved the fact that while we might be fierce rivals on the pitch, we'd all shake hands afterwards and congratulate each other on a great pass or try. It had been my experience that on the soccer pitch, if you scored or tackled, you wouldn't sit down and talk about it afterwards. After a rugby match, both teams sat down and ate together, which I think created the bonds and cemented the camaraderie.

The fact that the whole family could go to a rugby match also made a difference to the atmosphere. At the time, dads would be less inclined to bring their daughters to soccer matches, although that has changed for the better. In GAA and in rugby there is a really strong emphasis on getting children to play, something I don't see quite as much in soccer. And once you sign with a rugby club, that's it forever: in soccer, you move around much more, so it's harder to bring the family with you. In my opinion, women are more loyal, too: whereas a man will try to progress through club to club women tend to stay with one club and make friends there for life.

I craved that sense of family in sport and I found it in rugby. I can still remember that Anne would cook a big batch of lasagne and send me out the door, 'Go on, get out,' she'd say. 'I'm minding the kids so go and play your game.' I never worried when the kids were with Auntie Anne and I was free to just play. Jackie the soccer player was behind me and in her place was Jackie the happy rugby player, Limerick woman and eventually, Irish team member.

When I made the Irish rugby team in 1994, it was life-changing for me in so many ways. Des Byrne spoke to a local journalist and said, 'Look, I've got this player and she's making her debut at 33 and she's the first Black woman to play for Ireland and she's phenom-enal.' That was definitely an angle, as was my teaching the Irish national anthem to second-generation players. At the time, women of Irish descent who had grown up in England would often opt to play for Ireland, so it was left to me to teach them the Irish lyrics to our national anthem. The Black woman on the team was singing 'Sinne Fianna Fáil . . .' I had to do it all phonetically because of my dyslexia, but we'd practise it on the coach going to matches.

The journalist thought that this was great, but having the *cúpla focail* meant a lot more to me than a headline in a newspaper. It meant that I was accepted by my country. That I belonged. I wasn't the little outcast of just two months old, not good enough to be raised by my own mother. For the first time since I'd been with Fiona, I felt a real sense of belonging. After the interview, I went to the club for training. I can still remember that the snow was coming down and when the ball was kicked high into the sky, it disappeared into the flakes of snow. It was magic.

In the dressing room, I said, 'Listen, a journalist interviewed me today about my debut for the Irish team.' I filled them in and they started taking the mick out of me, Grainne Cross in particular. Grainne was some sportswoman: she'd played soccer for Ireland and Italy as a semi-professional and now she was a terrific rugby player. I used to joke that she was the most famous person I knew. Now, she teased me that the roles had been reversed. I admit I enjoyed the attention even if I didn't take it all that seriously, joking, 'I might become a star, you know.'

At the time, I was still working in the pub, cleaning the toilets, and coaching and working in Moyross as a youth leader, as well as playing my rugby, so I was busy, to say the least. One morning when I was cleaning the loos in the pub, the phone rang and it was for me. My first thought was, *has anything happened to the children?* 'It's the Pat Kenny show,' the owner, PJ, said to me.

'PJ, that's the girls playing a joke on me since I did that interview. Go and hang up,' I said, returning to squirting the rim of the toilet bowls with bleach. He strolled off to tell whoever it was that I was working. There was a long silence before he roared up the stairs, 'That's the chairman of Old Crescent and he asked me what you were doing about the Pat Kenny show.'

In a state of shock, I went down the stairs and picked up the phone. 'I've been trying to get you all morning,' the chairman said. 'They want you on before 11.'

'Why?'

'Did you not read the newspaper?'

'What newspaper?'

He tutted and ordered me out to get a copy of the paper. I walked out onto the busy street and into the newsagents, to see a photo of myself on the front of *The Star* newspaper. TWO-PAGE WORLD EXCLUSIVE the headline announced. But it was the article itself that worried me. I had proudly told them that my father was an All-Ireland champion handball player. Fine, but then I'd added, 'My mother is from Limerick, my father is Jamaican.' They got it mixed up and made the assumption that my dad, Mickey O'Brien, was Ireland's first Black handball champion. They'd even sent a photographer out to take pictures of me and the kids at home and at Thomond Park. I had thought nothing further about it until now. 'In a voice as smooth as a creamy pint of Guinness, this Black Irish woman is teaching her teammates the national anthem,' the article informed me. 'She is a scrummy lady!' it added.

Oh no, I thought. *I'll have to make this right.* So, I went back inside and called the Pat Kenny show, leaving my parents' phone number for them to call me there. Pat came on the line and in spite of my nerves, we chatted about my success. 'And what did your father think about being the famous Jamaican handball player?' Pat joked.

'Oh, he only laughed,' I said, which was true. I still have the article.

At an age when most sports people were retiring from sport, I was making my international debut, against Wales in Bridgend in 1994. I loved it and because of my speed, the manager moved me from the second row to the number-eight position, just like my hero, Anthony Foley, RIP. I had more freedom at number eight and I loved playing at the top of the ruck. Also, it helped that you don't have to be huge to do that job. Most of the other players would have been bigger than me, but I held my own.

I used to pretend to the others that I did weights but in fact, I never did. I didn't fancy all that muscle turning to fat when I retired, and I felt that my tall and thin shape was what was natural to me. I never got into the protein shakes and the weight-lifting and thanks to the Mount, I wasn't a big eater. I knew that in order to build muscle, I'd have to change my diet and it didn't feel right for me: after all, I'd got through 13 years of soccer with the body God gave me. In rugby, it's all about technique, not size. You can be the biggest player in terms of size and you can be pushed off a ball if your technique or stance isn't right. Of course, if one pack is much bigger than another, they'll have an advantage, but if the smaller team has a better technique, they'll come out on top.

The success of the women's rugby team soon caught the attention of the public and in particular *The Late, Late Show*. The show had heard the interview on Pat Kenny and we were to play our first home game in Limerick, so the night before the match we drove to Dublin to appear on the show. I was taking the manager with me, which nobody wanted! It's like driving with your boss, but he kindly offered to drive back down to Limerick so the arrangement suited me.

I always remember my mother and father giving out to me when I got home, because when Gay Byrne had asked me questions, I'd replied with a simple 'Yes'. I was stricken with nerves to be honest, like a deer in the headlights. In fairness, the questions only required a yes or no answer. 'So, Jackie O'Brien, you're making your debut for Ireland,' he asked me. 'Yep,' I replied. I didn't know that my mother and father had the whole of Limerick watching the show that night.

When I got back, Dad said, 'What was with the "yep"?'

'I was just shy, Dad,' I replied. Something about the bright lights and the focus of the audience had brought out my old shyness, but Gay managed to make light of our appearance. 'So, who's the hooker?' he said. It was an old joke but it put us at our ease. I can still remember one of the guests saying, 'You all look far too pretty to be on a rugby team.' To which my captain replied, 'That's because of all the mud baths we take.'

We got back to Limerick at two o'clock in the morning and we were playing England later that day. They were a very experienced team, who'd all been playing for a lot longer than us, so it would be a tough match. Limerick did us proud with three thousand spectators turning up to watch us play – and lose 0-32. That was a great result, believe it or not: the previous time we had played against England, they had beaten us 0-100, so this was progress. I can still remember coming off the pitch and my whole family was there to see me play. There were claps on the back of commiseration, and lots of people commending us on our performance. *That's what an international should be like*, I thought. Thousands of people out to see a women's team play.

Then Dad pulled me aside. I said, 'Well, what do you think? I know we got beaten and we need to do better.'

'You did well. They're at it longer than you and they're more professional, but you'll get there.' Then he added, 'But there's one thing you did and I'm disgusted with you.'

'What?'

'Your scrum-half squared up to one of the English players.'

'She did, Dad, but she was wrong. She was getting in fisticuffs with the English player.' I remember that the Irish player had faced the English girl down and we'd pulled her back, urging her to get back to play.

'Never. Ever,' he said sternly. 'I taught you that your teammates are your teammates: when one of them goes, you all join in, whether she's right or wrong. Wrong is for the dressing room – you do not do it on the pitch. You should have stood by her instead of pulling her away.'

That was Dad. He'd give credit where it was due, but if he saw something he didn't like he'd just say it. I knew where he was coming from to a certain extent. If you have not got that team spirit, you lose the essence of who you are as a team. You can go into the dressing room and say, 'you were completely in the wrong,' at half-time, but you don't do it in front of the crowd and you definitely don't do it against the opposition. If you do, you're showing your hand. Even if it was wrong, we should have stood by her. That's team spirit, that's team building, that's being a family. That's what stayed with me from that day, what Dad said to me. I watch Munster play now, and they'll all go in and the fists will be flying but a team's a team.

I went on to pick up a further 13 caps during my five years playing rugby. I took part in the European Championships in Nice in 1996, which was a revelation to me: I hadn't travelled much, so it felt as if a whole new world was opening up to me. By the time the World Cup would come along two years later, I was 38 and the manager thought I was getting a bit long in the tooth. I was still super-fit, but there was a chance I wouldn't make it. So, instead of dropping me from the team altogether, he selected me to captain the Irish 'A' team. I was disappointed, I won't lie, but it was still a huge honour to play for my country and to get match experience in the run-up to the World Cup.

What was ironic was that, as captain of the 'A' team, I would have been in on meetings about player selection, but when it came to my own selection, I had to leave the room. I had no idea whether I was going to be selected. I remember that when we were being selected for the Irish team, the manager had asked each of us, 'what is your ambition?' And all the players had replied that their ambition was to play at the European Championship or in the World Cup. My answer? To play just once in Thomond Park. 'That's the spirit,' he said. 'That's what makes for a great team player.'

I was getting older and I knew sport would come to an end for me, so about six weeks before the World Cup, I told the manager that I'd be retiring after the tournament. I had played a big match for Old Crescent and I had got injured but I was looking after it. I hadn't told anybody about the injury because I knew that it would end my chances of playing in the World Cup. However, I remember going to the gym for a swim one day and a woman stopped me in the street. She told me that she was a medium. I tried not to look too sceptical, but what she said as we were parting shocked me: 'Look after your foot. Oh, and that thing you're worried about making, well, you'll do it.' And then she walked off, leaving me open-mouthed behind her.

CHAPTER 16

FIELD OF DREAMS

People often ask me what the main difference was between my soccer and rugby playing days, and I'd have to highlight homophobia as key. When I began playing soccer, it was rampant in the game both here and in the UK. To this day, gay players are few and far between, at least publicly and the stereotypes about gay people are more visible. I would say that in rugby, the attitude is more nuanced. Yes, there might be homophobia, but in the main, it is less obvious, and players like Wales's Gareth Thomas and New Zealand's Campbell Johnstone have done a brilliant job at being ambassadors for the gay community.

In my own case, I started playing soccer in the 1980s and rugby almost fifteen years later, so attitudes in general had changed, but I do think that rugby is more open to gay players, and more about enjoyment of the game, rather than who you are and where you come from. In my experience as a rugby player, the attitude was that we were Irish Internationals first and foremost and we'd be treated as such. My sexuality never came into it and being the first Black woman on the Irish team, wearing the green jersey for my country, was celebrated. Having said that, we still paid our own way! The women's team was recognised by the IRFU, but not yet fully affiliated, so we all had to pull together to make things happen.

Meanwhile, I still had my foot to worry about. Every time I hobbled to the physio, I thought about the medium and what she'd said about me 'making it'. Could she mean the World Cup? I wasn't sure, but I also wasn't telling anybody how bad it was. I'd pulled muscles in my ankle and I knew that it was badly sprained. I'd iced it and strapped it as well as having physio, but I was out of training for the couple of weeks before the World Cup. I needed to play, but I needed to rest the ankle more.

Then the strangest thing happened. Just two weeks before the tournament, the manager left. Apparently, there had been some form of disagreement, but the assistant coach came in and took his place. What I later found out is that I hadn't been on the manager's list for the tournament – but the assistant manager selected me. Clearly, the meeting with the medium had done something.

When the letter arrived, I opened it with shaking hands. All I could see were the words 'You have made the international squad for the World Cup 1998.' The rest of the letter was a blur: 'Please be at such and such a place at the end of the day with your boots, your shin guards, your mouthpieces, your white shorts, your green socks . . .' The jersey would be supplied.

I was on cloud nine. This would be my final tournament wearing the green jersey, and what a way to go out, I thought, as I packed my bags to head to the tournament location in Amsterdam.

When we arrived, I was amazed at the professional setup. I'd come from a time and place where a couple of pints after a match was normal, as was eating whatever we liked. Now, we followed a strict regime from the start. We all got up and ate together as a team and we watched what we were eating: our protein and carb intakes were carefully monitored. I found that I had to eat more than I was used to, but the food was calibrated for maximum efficiency and this was new. Afterwards, we had a strict schedule. If we weren't training, we might have to appear at an event, in which case, we were instructed on what to wear, tracksuit or team uniform. Even though 'uniform' might simply be a polo shirt and tracksuit bottoms, we were all expected to wear it with no exceptions. There was no drinking allowed, either on the day of or after matches. If we didn't turn up for team meetings on time, we'd be fined. We were to be a well-oiled machine, utterly professional.

There were forty of us in the panel, so the selection process for the senior and 'A' teams was very competitive. The 'A' team were talented players, who needed match experience in order to make the senior team and I was to be captain. It was a great honour, even if I would have loved to be on the senior team. I couldn't really expect that though because of my injury.

During down time, we were often hanging around, so we'd break the boredom with silly games like choosing a word that couldn't be used on that day or having to wear a soother if you said a particular word. It was all good fun. There was a swear jar, of course, with the money going towards props, such as a plastic moustache or a dunce's hat. At the end of the tournament there was a mock court as well, in which players would be accused of harmless things and 'charged' accordingly. One woman was always on the phone to her husband, so she had to wear a telephone receiver strapped to her hand for one night! It wouldn't work with mobile phones, I suspect. The rest of the time, I spent with my roommate and it was fun to answer her frank questions about race and Black people's experiences. I wasn't often asked, but when you're together for long periods of time, sharing a room, you get to talking about things at a deeper level.

When the tournament itself began, it was like a roller-coaster, both physically and emotionally. I was happy just to be there because I was coming to the end of my career, but of course, once I'd arrived, I wanted to play, to be part of the team and really get stuck in. Being on the pitch is the thing you need and want, even as a sub.

During our first match, against Australia, I didn't get on at all. I was a bit down about it, but I was sure I'd get my chance. Australia were a fantastic team, way ahead of us back then. They beat us, but we left with our heads high. We did one unusual thing during that match: we had a fifteen-woman line-out and we pushed over the line to score a try against Australia. With all the cheering, you'd think we'd won the match. It gave us a lot of confidence.

For the next match, I made it onto the first 15, which I was delighted about. We were to play Kazakhstan. Now, this team were huge and they battered and bruised us, and we lost 6-12. We had moved from 16th seed in the tournament to 8th which was a great achievement. If you lost your first match, you went into another group called the Bowl. At the time, the women's game was more advanced in countries like England and Australia, so we'd have been hammered by those teams, but this system gave us a chance to play lots of matches and to test ourselves against other countries who were on our level.

Because I'd played in the match against Kazakhstan, I was really upset not to be selected for the panel against the Netherlands in the quarter finals of our group and we won this match. But again, you have to be professional, to suck it up and take it. Next we played Italy and won again, 20-5. In the Bowl final against Kazakhstan, I came on as a sub and I scored a try, which was absolutely brilliant. They beat us in the end, but we went from 16th to 8th in our seedings, which meant that we'd take that ranking into the next tournament. What was most important for me, however, was the experience.

At the end of the tournament, after the very last match, we assembled and sat in a circle, congratulating one another on our achievements, the wins and the tries, everything. And then I said, 'Look, it's been a pleasure and an honour to do this, but this is my last hurrah. I'm retiring from international rugby.' The girls were astonished and there were lots of pats on the back and good wishes, as well as slagging. But after the meeting, the coach came to me and said, 'Look, Jackie, you're making a decision at a time when everybody's exhausted. Think it over.'

I shook my head. 'No, I'm happy to leave knowing that it's on my terms. I'm happy with what I have achieved and I'm happy for somebody else to wear the jersey.' I meant it. It was time to hand over to younger women so that they could take the game forward. That was the only way we'd progress. I'd had my moment and I'd loved every bit of it. The World Cup was just the icing on what had been a wonderful cake.

I never regretted my decision. I played club rugby for another year, with Shannon Rugby Club, which made me very happy. And best of all? I got to play my final match at Thomond Park. We got to the finals of the All-Ireland club league and the match was in a place that meant so much to me. From childhood, I'd listened to the roars of the crowd on match day, or sneaked in to watch Munster play and now, I would walk out onto the pitch for the first and last time.

When I came back, I threw away my rugby boots as a symbol of the fact that I was done. That was it. I'd achieved everything I needed to achieve. There was nothing more to be done. I had gone from the ages of 11 to 40 playing soccer and rugby, so I knew that I'd given all that I could. Most people will play 13 or 14 years, but I'd been lucky enough to play for 29 – that's a very long time. And I have no regrets. It went the way it went. Perhaps I'd have liked to have had more time in rugby but I didn't regret the way my rugby career happened. I would have skipped the last years of my soccer career, possibly, but that's life. Rugby had restored the joy I felt in sport and that was hugely important to me. And to this day, I will bump into a boy or girl and they'll remind me that I'd coached them and they've gone on to play for great teams and that gives me a great kick.

Still, with Munster Rugby on a high, there was no further need for ambassadors to go into schools and encourage the kids to play. The kids were flocking to the sport now, of their own accord and I'd like to think that I played some part in that.

The question for me now was, what'll I do next?

CHAPTER 17

A NEW DREAM

I first met Lesley, the woman who was to become my partner for 18 years, in 1997. We'd bumped into each other at a bar and to make conversation she said to me, 'Oh, you're the famous basketball player.'

I wondered if she was joking. I'm tall and Black, but there the similarities end! It turned out that she'd seen my photo in the paper and not being sporty, had got rugby and basketball mixed up. In spite of the mix-up, we felt a spark between us, but even though Lesley gave me her number, I didn't call her back. I was very wary of introducing people to my children because they'd been so hurt when Fiona and I had broken up. If another relationship ended, it would be a loss for them as well, so there was a lot to think about.

But the fates must have intervened because two weeks later, I bumped into Lesley again. 'I was expecting a phone call and I didn't get any,' she said to me, half-jokingly.

I explained the situation to her and she understood. She was a mam too and she knew the complexities of dating when children were involved. We had both married and had our families young, so we were on each other's wavelength.

She said, 'Okay why not do things the old-fashioned way? We'll go on dates.'

I agreed and over the course of the next six months, we met up when our children were out with their dads. We'd go for walks and listen to music and cook each other food. It turned out that our children knew one another from soccer and socialising generally – Limerick is a small city – and they moved in the same circles, but even so, I wanted to take things slowly. I would head up to Lesley's home on the north side of the city at weekends when her kids were staying with their dad, or she'd come out and spend some time with me in Meelick. I'd pop in after work or training and she'd do the same, but we were careful to keep the children out of things, particularly as while I was openly gay, Lesley wasn't. Neither her family nor her friends knew so she was in a very different place to me. I was Jackie, her friend.

Funnily enough though, after a few months, it was Lesley who wanted to push the relationship along; I was happy with the pace of things as they were. Things came to a head when we went away to a wedding in Lahinch. I'd invited Lesley along as my plus-one and we had a lovely evening. Then before the night was over, Lesley took me aside and said, 'Right, this has been going on for six months. Are we officially in a relationship or not? I have plenty of friends. I don't need one more.'

I decided then and there. 'Do you know what? We're going to do it.' It was 31 August 1997, the day Diana, Princess of Wales died. Like everyone else, I was devastated at her sudden death in a car accident in Paris. I cried my eyes out over breakfast. It seemed unbelievable. Like so many women at the time, I had lived my life in parallel to hers: I'd been married to an older man, we'd had our children at the same time and my marriage had failed, just like hers. In other ways, my life was very different to hers, but I related to the way that she showed her vulnerability. That she'd loved her husband and he didn't love her back was, I think, something that so many women could relate to. She may have been royalty but we were all human.

Lesley and I knew that we'd never forget 31 August as the anniversary of our relationship, but we'd also celebrate on St Patrick's Day, to remember meeting up again. Now, we were official. We were committed to a relationship and loved each other deeply. Once I decide something, I'm full steam ahead. If we're doing it, we're doing it has always been my philosophy. Marriage wasn't open to us, but moving in together was, so that's what we'd do. I had more or less lived with Fiona so to go back to living apart from my partner wasn't what I wanted. I wanted to be gay and to be accepted openly: I had fought the fight when it came to my racial identity – I wasn't going to do that again.

Moving in together was hard – really hard. Blending together two families is not easy, so we decided that we'd each sell our homes and buy one house together closer to Limerick city that would fit all of us and make it possible for us to make a fresh start. We bought a doer-upper, and over the next couple of months we put all of our furniture in the garage, we put a mattress down in one bedroom, with a little hob to do a bit of cooking, or make a cup of tea and we started to renovate the house.

I loved the process. It reminded me so much of my own mother holding great sheets of wallpaper in her hands, neatly folded, to decorate the living room. My father, too, had taught me everything he knew about DIY, and I was so much of an expert at this stage that the following year, I decided to start my own business as a painter and decorator along with my friend, Caroline. We called ourselves Black and White Painting and Decorating and we got such a kick out of people looking at the van with the sign on it and realising one of us was Black and one was White! We got lots of business from the outset from women on their own who were happier to have other women in the house. It would also lead to a whole new dream emerging in my life, one that would become very special to me.

Lesley and I worked day and night to get the house ready for our family. They ranged in age from 8-16 at this point, so they were very much in and out of the house. My youngest, Stacey, moved in with my mam and dad, Lesley's children were living with her parents and Samantha and Robert were living with their dad for a bit. It felt as if we were building a new nest for our brood. It was a big, four-bedroom house with a garage, two sitting rooms and a large garden, so it was ideal. We went to town on it, with a theme in every room, complete with Egyptian-style bathrooms, a Gothic living room and an Eastern-themed dining room. We wanted to create something special, something memorable for our new life together. It was such a happy time for both of us.

When the house was finished, some of our combined families moved back in and some remained with grandparents, which we respected, even though we would have liked them to enjoy this new phase of our lives with us. My two younger children, Robert and Stacey moved in with us, along with Nora, Lesley's daughter.

Lesley and I had different perspectives on being parents. I would be strict about Nora having a boyfriend in the house and Lesley would be much more relaxed, possibly because she felt guilty and didn't want to rock the boat. I think her attitude was that Nora was suffering because of Lesley's decisions and so she felt bad about that.

Looking back, I wonder if I could have been a bit more flexible, because sometimes it would feel that Lesley was stuck in between Nora and myself. I could have picked my battles a little bit more. I saw Nora's challenging me as deliberate at the time, whereas now I wonder if she was simply finding it hard to come to terms with her mam being a lesbian and in a relationship with a woman. She'd also had her mother to herself for a good while and now, here was a whole new family landing in on her. She was testing the boundaries.

My children found it easier to accept my new relationship because of Fiona but what was interesting is that when we settled down a bit we soon settled into parental roles with 'Daddy' and 'Mammy' jobs. I would have been more of a dad, I suppose: a lot stricter about Stacey going out to discos, so Stacey would often approach Lesley first to smooth the path. Lesley would then come to me and negotiate.

Stacey and Nora soon grew into sisters, but while Stacey was only ten, Nora was 14 and I didn't want Stacey growing up too fast. Stacey's logic was that if Nora could do something like have a boyfriend at 14, then she could do the same when she was 14, which I didn't agree with at all.

Our differences were a real issue, early on, almost to the point of us breaking up at one point, but eventually, we bedded in and things began to settle. My work was a success and I was able to treat Lesley to nice things which made me very happy and when Lesley got a job as a teaching assistant in a local school, it seemed we'd got over that initial speed bump and the road ahead was smooth. And then another dream came into play, one that would shape our lives for the next decade.

CHAPTER 18

CONNEMARA

I can still remember the very first time I saw the mountains of Connemara rising up in the distance. It was a spring day in early 2000, and Caroline, my business partner and I were driving towards the village of Leenane and we came up to the top of a hill outside Clifden. The whole range of the Twelve Bens and the islands lay out before us, huge purple and green peaks rising in the distance. The sea was blue and sparkling and seemed to stretch away forever towards America. I couldn't believe such a place existed.

Caroline and I had come to do a painting and decorating job that was only supposed to last a couple of weeks, but we ended up spending a couple of months there because the project was huge. It was deepest winter and we were staying in a little cottage nearby that in spite of the heaters provided, was freezing. We'd wake early to throw our clothes over the heater to get them warm, then we'd get up and put them on as quickly as possible.

I can still remember the first time I was enveloped by the pitch black darkness there. We'd been working from early morning and hadn't notice the time passing. By eight o'clock, a heavy darkness had fallen. There wasn't a streetlight to be seen and we had to make our way home by torchlight, feeling our way the three hundred metres between the house and the cottage. We could hear a stream gurgling away in the darkness as our feet crunched over the gravel and every slight noise caused one of us to scream in fear. By the time we found the cottage, we collapsed in giggles at our city ways. We ate our dinners huddled over the stove, before waking early the next morning to repeat the long day.

By the time the job was finished, I'd fallen in love with the place. A Limerick girl through and through, my idea of a long trip was to head with the children to the beach at Lahinch and I loved the Burren, but Connemara was something else: there was something really magical about it. I knew that this was my place. I think everyone has a special place, one that they go to, to be themselves and Leenane was that place for me.

I quickly introduced it to Lesley, who was as blown away by it as me and we found a little cottage to rent so that we could spend more time there. To this day I love standing on the edge of Killary Harbour, with the mountains rising on either side of me, watching the boats heading out into the fjord.

We soon found ourselves spending every available weekend in Leenane, making the long trip up from Limerick on a Friday and returning on the Sunday evening. Thanks to the generosity of the man whose house we were decorating, we had somewhere to stay, and we'd all bunk down with sleeping bags and a little camping stove. Caroline and I even ended up painting in Ballynahinch Castle, which was truly memorable. The owner at the time wouldn't hear of us eating breakfast in our bedrooms, and insisted we come downstairs to the dining room, to share in the spectacular view of Benlettery and the lakes.

One day, a guest came to admire our work on the Victorian windows. 'That's very intricate work,' he said.

'Ah, we're experts at this stage,' I shot back happily. It was Seamus Heaney and he would later write the poem 'Ballynahinch Lake' in honour of the place. *Imagine*, I thought to myself as I worked, *Seamus Heaney was interested in us painting the windows*! But he was a lovely man. Painting in Ballynahinch and meeting Heaney reminded me so much of Dad and his love of poetry and my lovely teacher Rita Spring who had nurtured my own love of the form. It seemed to me that life had come full circle in the best possible way.

Soon, the dream of a place of our own began to take shape. Lesley and I began to discuss what this place might look like and what we'd do there. 'Maybe we could have paying guests,' I said. 'You could cook for them and I'd do the tidying and cleaning and picking them up from the airport.' Lesley was an excellent cook and we dreamed up a menu of traditional Irish favourites: bacon and cabbage, freshly baked soda bread, fish and seafood fresh from the harbour . . . I even dreamt of buying and breeding wolfhounds, because I've always loved the breed.

Plenty of people have a dream like this, and for many of us, it remains a dream, but as with everything I do, once I decide on something, I go for it. I thought that Lesley shared my enthusiasm: we'd have long chats about menus and day trips, but maybe for her it was just daydreaming and she didn't see it becoming real in the way I did. I was full steam ahead on making my dream come true.

In our naïveté, we thought we'd find an old cottage in the heart of Connemara for almost nothing, but of course, as a busy holiday spot, they were not cheap. And what's more, planning permission was hard to get unless you could prove that you were planning to live in a property, not just rent it out or use it as a holiday home.

And then we met Michael Keane. A local man, he was a gentle giant with hands like shovels and a lovely, soft manner. His uncle had left him his home on a bit of land a couple of miles outside Leenane. Michael was farming the land but had no use for the little cottage that had been his uncle's home. It was beautiful, with 360-degree views of the Twelve Bens. The cottage had been built to accommodate the workers bringing electricity to rural Ireland. With a cosy sitting room in the middle, it had three little bedrooms leading off it and from the front garden, you could see right the way down to the village and to Killary Fjord. Michael was happy to sell, but he didn't want 'people that were going to be moaning about the sheep', as he put it, which made me laugh. He didn't want it to become a holiday home, empty for most of the year. He also liked the fact that Caroline and myself were hard-working women, so he agreed to sell the cottage to me. Initially Caroline was to come in on the mortgage but a change of plans meant that it was now down to Lesley and me.

I fell in love with it from the moment I saw it. A couple of miles outside the village over a stone-built bridge, the mountains so close that you could almost touch them, it was perfect. All Lesley and I had to do was to find a mortgage to renovate it. In the days before the vacant home or derelict building grants, no bank would give us enough to renovate the place, so it looked as if our dream was in tatters. I went to Michael and said, 'Look, the bank will only give me eighty-five thousand pounds and that's not nearly enough to buy it and to do it up.'

'Sure what's the problem?' He held out his hand to me. 'It's yours.'

'Hang on,' I said. 'There's something else.' The bank wouldn't allow us to draw down the mortgage until we had some essential work done.

At this, he just smiled and stuck his hand out again. 'Sure I'm not asking you for money now, am I? Go and do it.' We shook.

'You're crazy,' my solicitor said to me when I told him about the deal. 'It's his house until you buy it. You could do it up and he could take it back then.'

'We've shaken hands on it,' I insisted. I knew that I could trust Michael and I was right. It took a year to get that cottage into a mortgageable state and not once did Michael approach us with a change of heart. What a gentleman.

We spent weeks and weeks in Leenane, stripping woodwork and painting walls, rewiring and replumbing. Renovating a house is a labour of love and you really have to want to do it to stick out the long, hard weeks of labour. Thankfully, Caroline and our other friends helped, coming down for the weekends to strip walls and pull down plaster. In the evenings, we'd all go down to Gaynor's pub and have our dinner and a few pints and a chat with the locals. It was such a happy time. And Lesley seemed to share my happiness, to love the place as much as me. I had even encouraged her to get into rugby and my beloved Munster and we'd go to matches together.

Looking back, did I ever sense that she wasn't fully into our lives in the way that I was? Later, I would have cause to question everything: every instance where she may not have shared my enthusiasm for something, but at the time, everything was going so well that perhaps I missed the signs. She and my youngest, Stacey, and myself formed a tight-knit unit, as the other kids began to grow and fly the nest. Robert moved out to live with his girlfriend and the others moved between us and their dads, as comfortable with them as with us. Caroline and I were busy with our business and Tom and I had managed to separate and remain good friends. What more could I possibly want?

CHAPTER 19

THE BEST-LAID PLANS

What is it they say about plans? That people make them and God laughs. It was 2006 and I was so invested in my dream, I had the whole thing worked out in my head. We'd buy another cottage in Connemara to do up and let out to visitors with the idea that we'd be able to work during the tourist season and live somewhere warm and sunny during the long winters. So when another cottage came on the market opposite Michael's place, I jumped at the chance to buy it.

I put everything I had into the second cottage, which needed a great deal of work. I used to joke that I had holes in my underwear, because I couldn't afford to buy new sets, even from the cheapest places. Every penny I was making was going in to the cottage. Lesley and I had an agreement about sharing the proceeds of any sale, and we were both happy with it. After all, we'd been together for nine years at this point, and I trusted her completely. We were both solid and with civil partnership on the way and, hopefully, gay marriage, we would be able to cement our relationship.

Looking back, it's possible I was so preoccupied with Connemara I didn't pay as much attention as I should have to my relationship. I was happy for Lesley to take the lead at home, because I loved her, but also, because I was afraid of losing her. In my mind, I would go out of my way to please her. On the other hand, when my dream of a new home in the west of Ireland took shape, I went at it all guns blazing – maybe I didn't see any hesitation on her part. Or maybe I didn't want to see it. We'd survived the upheaval of blending our families and everything that went with it and now, we could enjoy our lives together.

In the early days, Lesley's mam had not been happy with her divorce and her new relationship with me. When Lesley suggested, early on in the relationship, that she bring me home for Christmas, her mam had said she'd prefer if Lesley came alone.

Eventually, Lesley's father intervened. 'Look, you'll have to embrace this or you'll lose her,' had been his sage advice. To her credit, Lesley's mam did that and I ended up becoming part of the family. I have a habit of doing that, I know. I always want to belong, to feel accepted and loved and so I can overcompensate by offering to do anything and everything.

My parents had long accepted my sexuality, but whilst they liked Lesley, they had loved Fiona. They accepted Lesley, my mother making her a cup of her favourite milky coffee when she'd visit, but they found it harder to relate to her. Fiona had been very relaxed with them, enjoying the teasing and the banter but Lesley was more reserved. She came from a nicer part of the city than we did, so perhaps class came into it, but I always blamed myself for my feelings. I felt inadequate because of my insecurity.

Now there were subtle signs that things were changing. Lesley would drop me off at my parents' house and not come in to say hello. 'I'll just pop down and see my mam and dad,' she'd say.

Soon that became a regular thing. I wondered if she didn't feel comfortable with my parents or they with her. I can remember saying to Mam once that if the gay marriage referendum was passed, I'd marry Lesley. She didn't say much at the time, but when she'd mentioned it to Dad, he'd said, 'Sure what would you want to do that for? Why would you be bringing attention to yourself?' I think he worried that I'd been through enough with my identity and was afraid that getting married would give people who disapproved something to throw at me.

Marriage was something I really wanted: I wanted to tell the world that Lesley and I were together for life, that there was nobody else for me. Lesley was divorced but Tom and I were separated; it was time to make things permanent.

Tom and I had remained firm friends since we'd separated, so it was inevitable that we'd have the best divorce day ever. We were scheduled to attend court early one morning, but due to delays, we were told to go away and come back again later. 'Why don't we go out to Ardnacrusha?' Tom said. 'I've been painting a lot and you might like to see it.' Tom had always been creative and now, he'd got into painting and was creating all kinds of interesting work. We admired his paintings over coffee, before heading back to court. There we found that one case had run over, so our morning together turned into lunch in The Locke, a lovely gastropub by the river. We chatted easily about our lives and the kids like old friends – and we were old friends by this stage. We'd been separated for a very long time and our differences were all water under the bridge. Still, I wasn't prepared for what Tom said in court, when the judge asked him if he had any objections to our divorce: 'Well, it's what she wants. It wouldn't ever be what I'd want, but she's happy, so I'll gladly agree.' That really tugged at my heartstrings. In spite of everything, Tom and I were still family. It was a happy divorce and bittersweet at the same time.

We were a very modern family, I suppose. Tom was always invited to special occasions and helped out with odd jobs and I did some painting for Lesley's ex-husband. We'd even holidayed all together and we got on fine. The kids moved between us and their dads and everyone had a bit of space, so things really settled down. With everyone happy, Lesley and I decided to make the big move to Connemara.

In 2007, my life took an unexpected turn through events which I think would be wrong for me to chronicle here for the sake of the privacy of those involved. I found myself becoming a mum again at the age of 45; even though I had not intended to foster a baby, that's just what happened. A beautiful little bundle of joy came into my life, and at five months old, baby Kaya became my world. She needed me, just as I had needed Mickey O'Brien – here was history repeating itself. Now I understood just how much love you can have for a child that isn't yours by blood, just as my Dad had shown me.

Kaya gave me a new energy and a zest for life. I'd finish work earlier in the day just to have more time with her. As she grew up, walks about Limerick city became the daily routine for us, and I found I had a gift for storytelling, which she loved. She especially loved the stories about witches and fairies. I had bought Kaya a little fairy door for her bedroom and I would leave her little notes in the smallest handwriting I could manage, telling her how loved and protected she was. In turn, Kaya would leave notes for her fairy, and in those, I could understand how that little girl was feeling about everything – whether she was happy or sad about her school and her friends.

Just before Kaya's seventh birthday, Lesley and I were asked if we would be open to adopting Kaya, which we were. We were over the moon to do so. But events were to change that and I was to go on to adopt Kaya on my own in 2022. She is now 18 years old and in college, and I could not be prouder of the wonderful young woman she has become.

Back to 2008, Ireland's economy crashed and burned, the world fell apart. The first thing to happen was that Lesley lost her job as an SNA, due to government cutbacks. We'd deal with it, we thought. We'd move to Connemara and try to sell the second cottage to provide an income while we raised Kaya. It wasn't the way we'd planned a move, with a baby in tow, but life never really does work according to plan.

We spent the autumn in Leenane, watching the days grow shorter and the tourists disappear, the autumn winds whistling up and down the valley. It's not an easy time to go somewhere as remote as this, but I told myself that we'd be fine until the springtime, when the days would get longer and the weather better. I knew that this was part of living there, that the winters would be long, so I settled down to working on little jobs around the house and Lesley cooked meals and helped with Kaya. I didn't notice anything untoward about her behaviour – but then perhaps I wasn't looking.

We spent Christmas 2008 with Lesley's family in Limerick and perhaps this cemented her feelings, because when we returned to

Connemara for New Year, things were different. I knew that she was worried about her daughter, Nora, being so far away in Limerick. Lesley seemed distracted, her thoughts elsewhere. It all came to a head one afternoon when we were peeling potatoes. I watched her as she peeled and peeled, removing more and more of the potato until it was the size of a marble.

'Here,' I said. 'Let me help.'

With this, she dropped the potatoes and the peeling knife and burst out with, 'I'm sick of this. I'm going home. Please drive me back to Limerick.'

I was taken aback, but I agreed. She was probably just suffering from cabin fever, I thought, because of the weather. I drove her back, and I remember the weather was really, really bad: rain was pelting against the windscreen and the mountains had gone from their summer green to a dull grey-brown. It looked bleak. I saw it through Lesley's eyes for the first time and I wondered.

When we got back to Limerick, she got out of the car and went into her mother's, closing the door behind her. There was no real goodbye or 'see you later'. Bewildered and unsure what to do next, I drove back to Connemara with Kaya, back through the driving rain and wind. My thoughts were reeling. Perhaps she was just having a wobble and when the weather improved, she'd be okay. When I got to the cottage at last, it seemed chilly and bleak without Lesley and I couldn't imagine celebrating this New Year's Eve alone.

I called Mam and Dad in Limerick and they begged me not to stay by myself. As big celebrators of New Year, they were horrified that I'd spend it alone. 'Don't celebrate New Year's

Eve on your own. Come back up. Bring the baby with you,' Mam said.

I hummed and hawed before setting out at about three o'clock that afternoon. The temperature in Leenane was minus four and the wind was even colder than the previous day when I'd dropped Lesley back. As I left the steep hills behind me, I wondered when I'd see them again, before telling myself that it was silly. The Connemara dream was ten years old at this stage: all I needed to do was to talk it through with Lesley.

'Happy New Year!' I yelled when Lesley opened the door to me. I could see from her expression that she hadn't been expecting me. She led me into the sitting room in her parents' house and sat on the sofa, fidgeting.

'Surely this isn't the end?' I said to her. 'Why don't we talk and try to fix it?'

Finally, she blurted out, 'I don't want to live in Connemara.'

I was astonished. I knew that she'd been a bit down, but she'd never said that she didn't want to be there. This was the dream we'd shared since our relationship began. I didn't know what to say. 'Look,' she said, 'It's very different living there with a baby. It's lonely and isolating and I don't think I can do it. And our plan to go abroad for the winter months would not be easy once Kaya started school.'

I could see what she was getting at but I was shellshocked. I'd never considered anything else, so where did we go from here?

That night, I stayed in her mother's house and when we woke up, I said, 'Lesley, please, can we not sit and talk, maybe go to counselling?'

She shook her head. 'I don't want this,' she said. 'I don't want to go to Connemara.'

I knew that there was no point in trying to change her mind.

I left and I went out to Tom's with Kaya to see Stacey and her boyfriend. I ended up staying there for eight weeks, wondering what I'd do next. Caroline, my former business partner in Black and White, offered me my old painting job back and Tom said that I could stay for as long as I wanted, but I was inconsolable. Everything seemed to be ending: my dream, my relationship. I couldn't eat or sleep. The only thing that kept me going was looking after Kaya. Without her, I don't know what I'd have done.

Then Lesley started to come out and visit Kaya and we talked honestly and openly. 'Look, I don't think you'd ever be happy giving up your dream,' she said to me. 'But I can't do it with a small child, I'm sorry.'

'Okay then. I'll come back,' I said. Kaya was now the priority and it made sense to raise her in Limerick, close to family and friends. I knew logically that my dream of raising her in Connemara wasn't practical. I knew that I was doing the right thing in returning to Limerick: after everything Kaya had been through, it was for the best and didn't I love Limerick anyway? Kaya was thriving with us and with Lesley the homemaker and me going out to work again, we got a new rhythm in place and we seemed to be on firmer ground.

Stacey's then-boyfriend (now her husband) came with me to Leenane to pack up the house. I cried the whole time, boxing up Kaya's pram, our clothes, our pots and pans – everything. Stacey's boyfriend was brilliant. He put his arms around me and said, 'I don't know what to say to you. I know that your heart is breaking.'

And it was. But I thought, you know what? I just have to let it go. I have to move on. I have Lesley and I have Kaya and I should be grateful for what I have.

CHAPTER 20

ATTACHMENT DISORDER

Recently, I looked out of my window and I saw a little robin in the garden. *Oh, that's Daddy*, I thought. *He's come to see me.* My father died in 2012 and the following three years would be the most traumatic of my life. While everything was going on, I often thought back to my earliest years, which had been bleak, where I'd felt unloved and unwanted, but nothing could have prepared me for the losses that were to come.

That year started in the best way possible: Stacey's first child, Aaliyah, was born by Caesarean section and I was there to see her emerge into the world, folded in two like a little book. She was in the breech position, just as I had been – it must be a family trait! I was honoured to be there, and glad, because Stacey went into shock soon after the birth. She said to me only last week, 'Mom, I couldn't have done it without you. You rubbed my head like you used to when I was sick with my asthma.' I had – Stacey had bad childhood asthma and spent a lot of time in hospital. 'I just looked up at you and I said, "It's OK. My mam is there. Everything will be fine."'

Stacey was as keen on music as me, so she called her little girl after the late singer, Aaliyah. I used to call her my little frog because her legs were so tightly tucked up against her when she was born. But she was absolutely beautiful and we were assured that she was healthy. I was Nana Jackie and Lesley was Nana Lesley. The two of us had decided to start afresh with a move to Ardnacrusha, having spotted a worker's cottage in need of refurbishment. It was in a peaceful, tree-lined spot, on a small laneway that led away from the power station. The cottages had been built to house the workers who had built the hydroelectric plant and they were full of character but needed all the energy we had to do it up.

I had to pull a lot of strings and beg and borrow to buy the house: Dad gave me some of it, Fiona loaned me some more and the rest I secured by selling my brand new car at a knock-down price. It was all very difficult and stressful, as our home in Connemara was still for sale, so we couldn't get a mortgage on Ardnacrusha, but I was determined to pay for the cottage in full. It was agreed that Lesley's name would be on the deeds of our new home, as mine was on the Connemara homes. We got an architect to help us to renovate and to bring more light into what was a dark space, but while I was enthusiastic, I sensed that Lesley was less so. When I'd ask her if she liked a certain idea, a plan for the bathroom or our bedroom, she would say that it was fine, but little more.

After our eight-week separation, we'd patched up our differences and agreed to forge ahead together in Limerick, even if I felt a bit unsettled and my old insecurities, about not being enough for someone else, came to the fore again. I wondered if I was imagining her detachment or if it was down to me. At this point gay marriage looked as if it might become a reality and we agreed that as soon as it did, we'd be there. And Lesley was still wearing the commitment ring that I'd designed, so I told myself that it was all in my head.

Coincidentally, at this time, Lesley and I were to attend a parenting course run by the HSE to help Kaya with some issues she was having. She was a lovely little girl, but with Aaliyah's arrival, she began to show signs of distress, which were put down to something called 'attachment disorder'. We also knew that even though she loved crèche and being with other children, that developmentally, she lagged behind others in her age group. Lesley and I had done our very best to provide her with stability and safety, but the problems that had been there since birth needed to be addressed

As soon as I sat down in the room with a group of foster parents in a similar situation, the penny dropped. When the group leader began to define attachment disorder as a failure to bond with those who care for you, I immediately thought, *that's me*. I remember how distant I was from my mother when I first came out of the Mount, how I wouldn't oblige her by dressing up, or hug her easily, how I gave the impression that I didn't 'need' her, that I could manage just fine by myself. In relationships, I had been anxious and afraid to rock the boat in case the other person left. I put others on a pedestal and avoided conflict, refusing to walk away even when I knew I should.

The course taught me as much about myself as about Kaya. I began to get the sense that my feelings about my relationship with Lesley weren't the same as hers. But I didn't know how to talk it through without losing her, to the extent that I'd put Connemara away in a box marked 'holiday home', giving up on my dream without a murmur because I wanted so desperately for things to work out. Then I'd reason with myself that Lesley wouldn't be attending this course with me or talking about getting married if she wasn't invested in the relationship. It was all in my head, I thought, as we shared our stories with the group. Over the years, I have become an expert at compartmentalising: my relationship with Lesley would go into another box marked 'do not open'.

Then one Monday in the middle of April, I got a phone call from my dad. 'Listen, will you come and pick me up and bring me out to the hospital?'

'Sure,' I replied. 'Why?'

'Oh, your bloody mother made me go for blood tests last week.' I had to laugh, because Mam had always been 'the sick one' so to speak. She'd been in hospital quite a lot over the years and was prone to catching all kinds of things: I don't recall ever having brought Dad to hospital before that day – apart from arthritis, at 77, he was healthy and ploughed through everything.

Then he said something that worried me: 'So, the results have come back and I have to go out to the hospital.'

'Okay,' I said. 'I'll collect you in half an hour.'

When I drove up to the house in Kileely, he was standing outside, a small bag in his hand.

'What's that for?' I asked.

'They told me to bring a bag,' he said sitting into the passenger seat. My heart started to beat a little bit faster. *Maybe they were just taking him in for tests*, I thought.

We drove to the hospital, chatting away as we always did, even if I felt the anxiety build inside me.

When we got there, the doctor called us straight in to his office and sat us both down. He sighed and examined the file open in front of him on the table. 'Mr O'Brien,' he said gently. 'I'm afraid that the blood tests reveal that you have leukaemia.'

The shock almost floored me. I opened my mouth to say something, then closed it again. I looked over at my big, strong dad to see what he was thinking, but his face was impassive. The silence seemed to stretch on to eternity, before he said, 'Can we fight it?'

'Yes, we're going to fight it,' the doctor said. 'We'll have a battle on our hands, but we're going to fight it.'

So, it was treatable, I thought. It wasn't as bad as I'd imagined. I was in shock, but I knew that Dad would fight it. He was strong and he'd overcome so much. He'd be sick for a while, but then he'd be fine. One of Tom's nephews had had childhood leukaemia and he'd overcome it, so it was curable. *There is no way that my dad will die*, I thought.

The very next day, Tuesday, Dad had his first session of chemo, followed by another session two days later, and another two days after that. At the beginning, Dad sat up on the bed, a drip going into his arm, and chatted away to people. He loved a good conversation and his natural curiosity led him to make friends with everyone else on the ward. But by the time a week had passed, he was quieter. He didn't chat as much and he'd nod off in the chair. He didn't seem to have much of an appetite either.

It's just the effects of the chemo, I thought. I knew that the treatment was really tough, so I hoped that he'd rally, but with every session, he seemed to grow weaker. We began to worry: was this to be expected? My sisters, my brother and I gathered around worrying and wondering. Four weeks later, we got our answer. His white blood cell count hadn't returned to normal. He was in exactly the same spot as he'd been four weeks' earlier. The harsh treatment hadn't worked.

My sister, Regina, was livid. Why hadn't they left him alone, she fumed. Why had I gone along with the plan – he would have had an extra three or four years otherwise. I knew that this was unrealistic but in hindsight, maybe Dad could have avoided all that suffering for nothing. I'm sure many people feel that way, but even though I knew where Regina was coming from, we had a massive argument. I think she blamed me for the decision to go ahead with the chemo, but who knows what might have happened otherwise? I knew that it was grief talking, fear at losing our dad, but neither of us could see past it.

Then I heard Dad's voice: 'Jackie. Take me home. Just take me home.'

It was a Friday in spring, and through the window of the hospital, the weather was fine and sunny, all the trees out in bloom. Everything was growing, but my dad was dying. 'Look Dad, will you give me the weekend to organise your room and bed for you? We'll have to convert the shop space, because we won't be able to bring you upstairs.' Dad nodded quietly.

I made phone calls straight away to my cousins on the O'Brien side. They had always been there for us and they all came down to Kileely to help to convert the shop that had been his livelihood into a makeshift bedroom. We stripped out what was left of any shelving, we put up partitions, we plastered and painted and by the following Monday morning, we had it ready for Dad to come home.

It was such a quick process in the end. Within a week, we went from having carers come in morning and evening to the palliative care team arriving from the local hospice to prepare Dad for the final journey. The whole family gathered to celebrate Mam and Dad's 48th wedding anniversary, singing and telling stories. We called Mam's sisters in Birmingham to return home to Limerick to say goodbye. It was a time of mixed emotions: joy and sadness, as word spread of Dad's illness and everyone came to see him. We made a rota of children and grandchildren to sit with him so that he'd never be alone.

The palliative care nurse was lovely, but she'd seen people dying many times and one day she said to me, 'His heart is strong, but he's going downhill.' Then I knew: he wouldn't be with us much longer.

One morning, two weeks after he'd returned home, he was lying in bed, half asleep. I had come in and was giving him a pep talk: 'Come on, Dad, fight it. Don't give up.' I knew that I was being blind to reality, but I couldn't bear to think of him leaving all of us. I was sitting on the edge of the bed when he reached out and took my hand. He whispered, 'Just look after your mother.'

Mam had checked in on him earlier that morning along with Marie and Joan. 'Go into town with your sisters,' he'd urged her.

'No, I'm staying here,' she insisted but he stilled her with a look. 'Go on away into town.'

Mam sighed but knew better than to argue, so off she went into town. In hindsight, I wonder if Dad knew that this day was the day. As I looked at him in the bed, I had a feeling that it might be. I'm not sure why but something in the air had changed.

When a cousin of mine called to the door for an update, I turned to my brother Gerard and said, 'Don't leave him.' I said it to everyone that day, not to leave him alone for a second.

I went to the hall door to say hello to my cousin, Derek. 'Will you come in and see Dad?'

He shook his head. 'No. I don't want to see him like that. I have my vision in my head of Mickey O'Brien, the big strong man, and I want to keep it like that,' he said sadly.

Next thing, Gerard appeared beside me. 'Jackie, will you come in? I think he's gone.'

No way, I thought. *He wouldn't go without us all being there.* But he had. With Gerard by his bedside, he'd quietly slipped away.

I went into autopilot. Like a robot, I picked up a hand mirror and put it to his mouth. There was no shadow on the glass, so I knew that he wasn't breathing. I put my hand on his neck to check his pulse but could feel nothing. He was gone. I washed his face and then I put his false teeth, which had been taken out in case he'd swallow them, back in. *There's no way anyone is seeing Dad without his teeth.* I brushed his hair and then I thought, *what do I do next? I know, I'll call the doctor to come and certify the death.* Then it occurred to me: Mam. She'd gone shopping with her sisters – Limerick was a small place. What if word got out about Dad before I had the chance to tell her?

Dad had been gone for about half an hour and I knew that the bus from town was due in Kileely shortly. I stood at the front door, from where I could see the bus stop straight across the road until the bus pulled up and I saw Mam and her sisters getting off. I could hear her laughing with my aunties, the three of them carrying bags of shopping.

I stepped back a bit so she wouldn't see me immediately and I watched her cross the road and come down the path towards the garden gate. I was standing at the front door and the moment she saw me, she went, 'No, no, no!' The bags fell with a thud to the ground. I went out to meet her to put my arms around her but she pushed me out of the way and ran into Dad's bedroom. I can remember her saying, 'I knew you'd do it to me, Mickey. I knew you'd go when I wasn't here. You wouldn't make me say goodbye.' Her devastation was hard to hear.

Soon, the family gathered to sit with Dad. I volunteered to go to the undertakers to sort out the funeral arrangements. I was still on autopilot, sitting with the undertaker looking at pictures of coffins. It was only when he asked me if Dad would be reposing in the church the night before the funeral that I snapped into action. Absolutely not. Dad had a healthy disrespect for the Church, so there was no way on earth he would want to be removed there before the funeral.

Dad's issues with the Church had all started when Mam had lost her second child. The rule then was that unchristened children couldn't be buried on consecrated ground. Dad, being Dad, wasn't having it. He wouldn't let my mother go through that experience and have her child buried in a grave outside the cemetery, and so he hopped over the wall of the cemetery in Kileely and dug a little grave there himself. Word got around and if children died before they were christened, my dad was the person the parents would come to. He would climb over the graveyard wall and find a suitable place for them to be put to rest. He did this out of kindness and a kind of disobedience of the Catholic Church.

He didn't want it to dictate the fate of an innocent baby and so he took matters into his own hands.

I can't imagine that it was easy either to bury his own or someone else's child but that was typical of Dad – principled and unafraid. Thinking about it, my stay at the Mount probably influenced him too: he'd seen what the Church could do to a family and he didn't want it. Ironically, as I talked to the undertaker, my sister, Caroline, called. 'Jackie, the priest is after turning up to say a decade of the rosary.'

In my shock I blurted, 'Oh, for God's sake, if there's a priest there, Dad must really be dead.' I knew that he'd have kicked the man out otherwise.

We arranged for Dad to be waked at home, in the old shop where he'd spent so much of his life. The undertakers did a lovely job, but when he came back to us in his coffin, they had nicked his top lip with the razor while shaving him. Before he could be viewed, I asked my daughter Samantha's girlfriend if she would put a little bit of make-up on it to conceal the cut. She took out her concealer and in her attempt to dab it on, she gave him a very obvious moustache. We collapsed with laughter – the kind of nervous giggles that come on occasions like these.

In the end, we opened the door of the house for people to file into the shop and pay their respects, before going to his beloved handball alley for a cup of tea and a sandwich. Everyone in Kileely came, including Dad's two best friends Dom Kiely and Ger Walters. They were two big men and I'd looked up to them all my life and there they were in Dad's old shop, crying. It hit me again that Dad was gone. Really gone.

From four o'clock until eight o'clock that night, people came through the house and told us stories about Dad's kindness to them giving them credit and helping them out. One of them revealed that Dad and Mam were married within six weeks of first meeting, which really surprised me. The following day, Dad had to be taken to the local church. Lay ceremonies or humanist funerals weren't a thing yet, so finding something other than a Catholic service was hard. But if he was to be carried into the church, I wanted to do it. So myself, my brother and Dad's nephews carried him in.

After the Mass, I stood up to give the eulogy and as I always do when I'm nervous, I told jokes, funny stories about the things Dad had got up to, but also about how he gave up drinking and smoking and how much he loved his wife and family. The realisation of all the things that he had done for me came flooding back: the way he'd encouraged my sport, had given me my first job, had handed me the stick that day and invited me to hit my bully back as hard as I could, knowing that I wouldn't. 'You can fight all your life or you can get on with it.' Dad's wisdom. Even today I find his words coming back to me in moments of sadness or anxiety.

Afterwards, we stood in a line at the head of the coffin, Mam, my sisters and brother and my aunties Joan and Marie. Three ladies whom I'd seen at the wake and who hadn't spoken to me made a beeline for me. 'We're really, really sorry,' one of them said. 'We didn't realise who you were. We grew up with your dad and we left and moved to England and lost touch with him. Then you stood up and read the eulogy and it was pure Mickey O'Brien. You're just like your father.'

'You're just like your father.' I don't think I've ever received a nicer compliment. It really was a moment that made me feel, he's still here through me.

We had decided to bury Dad in St Mungret's Cemetery, which isn't the norm for Limerick people, but because there had been a lot of vandalism and theft from Mount St Lawrence, the city cemetery, we decided that we'd move him. I don't know whether it was a good thing or a bad thing, because on the day, the hearse drove along the road out of the city, taking Dad away from his beloved Kileely and all the familiar spots of his life. And when we got to the final stretch of road that led to the cemetery, it was closed off for roadworks. The hearse had to do a U-turn and come back and then we had to do a U-turn as well, passing the hearse with Dad inside it, his photograph in front of the coffin.

Dad wasn't a man who would laugh out loud. If he was told something funny, you'd see the tiniest twitch of his lips and his shoulders would begin to shake in a kind of inward laugh. In the photo in the hearse, he had that tiny smirk, as if to say, 'You eejits – you're taking me to the wrong place, you know.' Dad would have loved it. He would also have enjoyed the fact that the priest got lost on his way to St Mungret's and was half an hour late to bless the coffin. To cap the dark humour of the day, Dad's nephews had brought along two beautiful white doves to release in Dad's memory: when they released them, one of them came straight back down to earth, landing in front of us, stone dead. *Oh my God*, I thought, *Dad just does not want to be here: he's telling us something.*

After the funeral, the shop was thrown open again and it was like New Year's Eve, when all the customers would come for crubeens and whatever Dad had gathered in the way of drinks. It was a celebration of a man with a strong personality, who knew his own mind, was the soul of kindness and who made his mark on his community and on those who loved him.

One of my favourite Dad stories – and there are many! – sums the man up:

Dad bought some shelving for the shop to display fruit and vegetables. He bought them on 'HP' as we used to call it, where you paid off a loan over a certain number of years. In this case, Dad paid the loan off over five years and after five years, he stopped paying. The next thing, he got a letter saying that they weren't actually paid for at all. Dad had only been leasing them and now, the letter said, he had the option to buy them over another five years.

Dad saw red. He rang the shelving company and said, 'You know what? You can take them out.' The letters kept coming threatening court action if he didn't resolve the loan issue. He responded by telling them that he had now taken the shelving out – which he had. He'd dismantled it, put it in the store and he now invited them to come and reclaim their shelving. 'I am not buying your product,' he said firmly.

The reply was along the lines of, 'You've paid for a lease for five years and you still have the shelves.' As far as Dad was concerned, he didn't. He'd removed them and put them in the store, waiting for their collection. The letters continued to arrive, but Dad ignored them. He'd written to them to ask them to collect their shelving and that was the end of the matter.

One day, Tom and I were coming into town and we met Mam coming the other way. We stopped to talk to her. Her face was chalk white. 'Your father's been arrested,' she told me. The Gardaí had turned up on the doorstep to take him into Limerick Garda station to question him about the theft of some display shelves. He was being held in a cell, she said, like a criminal.

When Tom and I arrived at the station, we were allowed in to see Dad, who was sitting in a cell, the door wide open. It was clear that the Gardaí didn't believe he was a criminal, but it must have been really frightening for him. Still, Dad being Dad, when Tom and I offered to pay to resolve the matter he said, 'If you pay them, you need never darken my door again.' That was typical of Dad: a principle was a principle.

What could we do? Dad was transported to the court that day, sentenced to two weeks in jail and by the following morning, he was in a cell in Limerick prison.

Then the campaign started. His customers began to write to the court and soon a campaign was in full swing. 'Free the Kileely One' it was called. No councillor or TD was left out of the mailing list. The irony was that Dad enjoyed his two weeks in jail! For the first time in years, he could relax. He had nothing to do except lie around, putting on weight. When we'd visit him, he'd be in great form, telling jokes and stories about his fellow inmates. He even joked with my mother that he had a few new recipes for her, as her cooking wasn't very good!

After two weeks, he was brought up before the judge again and asked to pay for the shelving. 'Your honour,' he said. 'I've paid for it and that's the truth. I told them to take the shelving because I owe them nothing but if you feel prison is the best place for me, that's fine.'

The judge was incensed at the sheer nonsense of the case. He threw it out and Dad was free to go. That was my dad, a man of principle. He taught me everything I know.

After all of the busyness of the funeral and the arrangements, everyone went home. Mam's sisters went back to Birmingham, Dad's nephews returned to their families. There was only us left to mourn him and to look after Mam. To me, that's always the hardest time, when the house seems so empty and sad. I sometimes think that we want to do things too quickly in Ireland – we bury people within 48 hours of their passing, so there is so little time to come to terms with things before the real grieving begins. Then we have to do it alone.

We began to gather Dad's things together, just like every other family does when a loved one passes. We kept some of his possessions and boxed others up to be given away. Then I saw Dad's dressing gown on the back of his bedroom door. I'd given it to him one Christmas and I didn't want it to go to the charity shop, so I took it home and I put it on and it felt like a warm hug. To this day, when I sit in the kitchen drinking coffee or writing or making a video, I'll put it on and I'll feel that he's there with me, cheering me on.

Chapter 21

Losing Myself

After Dad's death in June 2012, I threw myself into renovating the house, but in spite of all the activity, I knew that his death had changed something fundamental in me. He had always been my rock, as well as my guide and mentor, and without him, I felt that I'd lost my grip on the little world I'd created for myself with Kaya and Lesley. I'd had a vision of making them happy by providing a nest for them, and that their happiness was all I needed, but now, I began to wonder if I was happy in myself.

Now that Dad wasn't there any more, I began to wonder what he'd think about the balance of my relationship. As the years had passed, I felt a gradual sense that I was losing myself. That my identity as Jackie, who played soccer, who loved to dance, to have fun, who knew what she wanted, had gradually disappeared. I rarely saw my old soccer or rugby friends and also rarely went to Connemara now that the dream of living there had ended. From being sociable and outgoing, I became dependent on Lesley for my social life. Also, I had changed from the achiever, the doer, to a person who gave to others to the detriment of herself. *What if I stop giving*, I wondered. *What would be given to me?* That thought and the thought of what Dad might think if he were here, changed me in a lot of ways.

I also began to develop physical symptoms of my grief. I had carpal tunnel syndrome and shoulder pains. I had a constant cough and at night, I'd grind my teeth, waking up in the morning with a sore jaw. I ended up having to have three of my teeth taken out. I think it was grief coming out in its own way. I also started to get kidney infections and one day at the GP's surgery I met an older woman who told me that the kidneys are related to grief. Blood tests would reveal that I had rheumatoid arthritis and I was given cortisone injections by the wonderful Prof Alexander Fraser, which settled my symptoms down, but I still felt tense and unwell, as if I was holding onto something inside me.

I realised that I was living my life through Lesley. I wasn't complaining because she looked after Kaya and the home so well, but I felt lost and lonely because I wasn't leading my own life. I was letting Lesley make the decisions about what we'd eat, what Kaya would wear and so on. Slowly, I began to test the boundaries, saying that I'd like to eat something different for dinner or that I'd prefer not to go out with her friends. I described them as my 'backbone moments'. I'd never done that before. In fact, I'd gone everywhere with Lesley, unless I was minding Kaya. Now, I longed to go out with my friends, but even though I was beginning to develop that backbone, I wasn't ready to make that leap.

I loved Lesley and I knew that she was a good mother to Kaya, but there were subtle changes. When Kaya was small, we'd used to lie in bed with her in the mornings and Lesley would get up to make breakfast for us and we'd all lie there, bouncing Kaya around, playing with her and telling her stories. That began to happen less and less. Lesley was getting up earlier and earlier and coming to bed later and later. I'd be in bed reading my book, waiting for Lesley to come in and to chat about the day but when she didn't appear I'd fall asleep. Then our intimate life began to suffer. It wasn't that I longed for it every night, but more that I felt it shouldn't disappear altogether. At this point, I remember having a chat with her and saying, 'Maybe we should go to counselling about this because this shouldn't be us at this age.' We were both only fifty. I was shocked when she told me that that wasn't something that interested her any more. What about the walks and the hand-holding and showing each other affection? I didn't think that I could manage without that closeness. I knew that Dad wouldn't be proud of the person I had become.

Also, the attachment course we'd attended for Kaya had had a big impact on me. One of the things that the counsellor had said was, 'Keep your child in your mind as you do this course.' I was keeping Kaya at the forefront of my mind, but I also saw myself as little Jackie. I started to see traits of attachment or detachment in me as clearly as I could see them in Kaya. I began to notice my low self-esteem and that desperation to be loved. I remember Kaya was always looking for attention, no matter whether it was good or bad; for me, I was looking for love. One of the big things that came out was when the counsellor said, 'Your [foster] children feel invisible, so they're constantly jumping up and down saying, "Can you see me? Can you see me? Can you see me?" They will do anything to get that attention, whether it's being told off or praised.' That really connected with me. I had felt invisible in a lot of ways as a child.

As I started to practise the exercises from the course with Kaya, I began to pay more attention to things like boundaries and choices. Instead of saying to Kaya, 'No, that's bold', I'd give her a choice: 'Right, Kaya tomorrow we're going to the park. If your behaviour is good, we'll be able to go, but if it's bad, we won't be able to do the things you want to do. It's your choice.' We were putting healthy boundaries in place for Kaya and giving her choices around her behaviour.

It suddenly dawned on me that I had no boundaries at all in my relationship with Lesley. If I ever attempted to put any in place, I'd break them and leave my heart and my feelings exposed. This shook me to the core. Where was I in my life? Who was I? I began to establish boundaries for the first time: after a row, I would always have been the first to go in and apologise, but now I decided to step back and reflect, to not jump to attention.

Even so, we still talked about getting married. Now, we were at a place where a referendum on gay marriage looked certain to be held, so I bought wedding rings and we both wore them. There was clearly something still holding us together. We had Kaya, and our precious dogs, Murphy, a miniature Schnauzer and Fionn, an Irish Wolfhound, and I told myself that things were still good.

It was now October 2014, and Dad had been dead for two long years. At the end of the month, we celebrated Lesley's 50th birthday. I got a lovely card and gave her the present of a flight to Texas to see her brother. We got cake and we got flowers and had a lovely family afternoon. Afterwards, Lesley and I went to a seventies night with my daughter Stacey and her boyfriend and we had a great time. For some reason, the DJ played Ed Sheeran's 'Thinking out Loud' and I held her close and told her, 'I love you and hopefully, this time next year, we'll be married.'

I can still remember that a woman saw us dancing and came up to us then and said, 'I've never seen two people so in love.'

It was ironic, because from that moment, our world fell apart.

A couple of days after her 50ᵗʰ birthday, Lesley stood at the end of the bed and said, 'I'm leaving.'

We were both getting ready for work. I had been about to go into the kitchen and get something, but I turned and said, 'You're leaving work?'

'No,' she said. 'I'm leaving. I'm done.'

The penny dropped. I just stood there, frozen with shock. Eventually, I said, 'Has something happened?'

'No,' she replied calmly. 'I'm just going.'

'Look, we'll talk about it when we get back from work,' I said, unable to think of any other response. I couldn't believe that she was serious. All day, I felt physically sick. I couldn't function. I rationalised what she'd said to me that morning. Maybe, I thought, she wants to go and look after her mam for a while, but all the while my stomach was churning with anticipation.

When we came home that evening, we sat down and we had the conversation. 'What is it? I said. 'Is it that you want us to spend more time together or . . .?'

'No. I don't want to be here,' she said. 'I don't want this lifestyle or to live out here.'

Ardnacrusha was a few miles from Limerick but it wasn't the moon, I thought. Still, that was easy to fix. We could find somewhere nearer. I was about to suggest it when she said, 'I'm going to Mam and Dad's'.

'What happens with Kaya?' I said.

'She stays with you. This is her home. My mother and father aren't able for a young child and they won't be able for Kaya.'

I was shocked. Lesley seemed so composed, so matter of fact, as if she'd made up her mind long ago and this was the end of a process, not the beginning. I remember thinking, *how will I manage this child on my own?* Lesley was the homemaker and minder – how would I be able to do it as well as working?

'Look, please don't leave until I speak to the HSE.' Kaya was still our foster child, so they needed to be informed.

Lesley agreed to stay for the next six weeks. I felt a bit better then because I thought that six weeks would give her time to change her mind, to see what she'd be losing if she left. But within a week or so, it became apparent that she wasn't going to change her mind. I started to notice that some of her things were disappearing from the house. She had already started moving out.

I hadn't seen it coming. I was absolutely devastated. I cried and cried some more, begging her to stay. This wasn't good because I'm sure Kaya could hear us through the partition walls, but I couldn't help it. I was little Jackie, begging her not to leave. 'Look, let's go to counselling,' I suggested, 'then we can sort this out. If we get to Kaya's birthday next March, things will look better then.'

Over the past few weeks, I'd kept asking her if she didn't love me anymore and she hadn't answered. Now, she said, 'I don't want to be with you. I don't love you and I don't want this life.' *This wasn't the same Lesley*, I thought. It was over. I had begged her on my knees to stay, but I knew that this was the end.

In the weeks that followed, the pain was unbearable. I could feel it physically, deep in my bones. I found it hard to sleep and the weight dropped off me. Kaya kept asking me where Lesley was going and why and I found it impossible to tell her the truth.

The HSE social worker called out to discuss our fostering of Kaya. 'Where do you see yourself in Kaya's life, Lesley?' she asked.

'I'll try to help out where I can,' was Lesley's response. It was as if someone had pulled down a shutter. We'd been the poster girls for fostering, the first lesbian couple to come into mainstream fostering. Through our example, the HSE was hoping that more gay couples would volunteer to foster. Now what?

When Lesley left, the social worker said to me, 'I can't believe that this has happened.'

For whatever reason, my mind took me back to the moment when Lesley told me all those years ago that she'd left her husband. To me, it seemed that she'd simply got a job, got an apartment, put a six pack of beer on the table, and walked out of his life forever. Maybe she'd been planning that for a while, too, I thought, or maybe it was that she could compartmentalise things. When she was done with a relationship, she was done. She made a clean break of things.

Lesley moved out to her parents and for the first couple of weeks, she'd take Kaya a couple of afternoons a week. She'd pick her up from school, give her dinner, help her with her homework and bring her back out to me. On those days, I'd work for a little bit longer, but other than that, I was taking Kaya to school, finishing work early to pick her up again, and doing what I had to do. I was like a robot, moving through my days on autopilot.

One day, I put some potatoes into a pot on the stove and left them on a low heat to cook while I dropped Kaya to school.

There I happened to bump into my sister, Caroline and we got talking. She'd been a great help to me with Kaya, picking her up from school and taking her to see my mother when I was at work. 'How are things?' she asked me sympathetically.

'Not great,' I replied. I could hardly get the words out, so I said, 'Listen, I've left the potatoes on the stove. I'd better run.' When I got back, smoke was billowing out of the pot in the kitchen, filling the house with a terrible smell. Holding my nose, I ran in to turn off the pot and toss it into the sink. And at that moment, I hit rock bottom. I remember thinking, *I can't even fucking boil a pot of spuds.* I dropped to my knees in front of the kitchen sink and cried my heart out. I thought, *how do I mind this child when I'm falling to pieces myself?* I had no idea. After a while, I wiped my tears with a tissue and I picked up the phone and I rang Lesley. 'You're going to have to come and take the child. I can't do it. You're better at this than me. I just . . . I've given everything I can, and here I am. I don't know who I am. I don't know how to function. I just don't recognise me. This house, this home, was all about you and Kaya, and you're not here. And the child would be better off with you.' At that moment, I can remember thinking, I'd be better off not here.

'I'll be on a break at 12,' Lesley said. 'I'll ring you then.'

The moment I put down the phone I thought, *Jackie, are you crazy? Remember the time when you took all those Anadin and you felt so selfish after when you realised what it would have done to your family. You're so selfish. Kaya needs you and your other children need you.* I got up, rinsed the burnt pot out, brushed myself down and thought, *Dad can see you now. What do you think he'd say? He'd tell you to get up and get on with it.* 'Get up and get on with it. Remember whose daughter you are. Remember everything you've been through.' I was so ashamed of having that thought, even for five minutes.

Needless to say, twelve o'clock came and went. Lesley didn't ring me. That was another revelation. I thought, *she hasn't loved me for a long time*. This isn't a fresh goodbye: it's been there for a long time. That realisation – and the one that Kaya needed me – helped me to accept that Lesley had left and was not coming back.

It was November now and the nights were getting longer. Kaya and I would curl up in my bed and we'd watch *I'm a Celebrity Get Me Out of Here*. We'd look at celebrities eating grubs and having rows in the Outback and it would comfort us both. Kaya missed Lesley: she'd been looked after, fed and cared for by her for the past seven years. I missed Lesley too, more than I could say and it helped us to get through it together.

Sadly, Lesley began to disappear from Kaya's life too. Once, when Kaya was coming out of school at home time, she bumped into Lesley. She was thrilled that Lesley had come to collect her, but when she found out that Lesley was picking up another child whom she'd agreed to mind instead, Kaya was devastated. She stood in the playground, hurt and angry until I arrived. That made me very angry, too, but I tried not to show it around Kaya.

One day, the social worker called to see how we were getting on. 'I sleep in Mummy's bed now,' Kaya told her. 'I only go to my mam's bed sometimes and we're watching *I'm a Celebrity* and they're all eating animal penises and testicles . . .' she said.

Oh my God, I thought, looking nervously at the social worker. When she saw the worried look on my face, she laughed and

caught my hand in hers: 'Jackie, whatever gets you through it.'
To this day, Kaya and I watch *I'm a Celebrity* together.

Kaya was seven when Lesley left and from that point, Lesley
didn't see Kaya on her own. There was always a family member
or friend around, as if she didn't want the intimacy of seeing
Kaya by herself. Perhaps she was afraid of the questions Kaya
might ask about her leaving, or that she'd ask when Lesley might
be coming home. After a while, Kaya came to resent the fact that
there was always someone there and she would ask to come home.
I didn't understand it. Until the day that she left, I would have
said that Lesley loved Kaya just as much as I did. Soon, Kaya
and Lesley's relationship began to crumble. Lesley felt that I was
in some way responsible, but I don't think that's true. I was a
self-employed painter and decorator who looked after Kaya 24
hours a day. I was happy for her to go to see Lesley. After all, I
knew that Lesley was the one person who would keep Kaya safe.
I don't think that Lesley realised that Kaya wanted her sole attention. Soon, Kaya stopped going to see Lesley altogether.

Again, the HSE called to see what was going on and Kaya told
them in her own words, 'I don't want to go. I want to stay with
Mummy Jackie.' Kaya became clingy and suffered from separation
anxiety. I saw all of the hard work from the attachment-disorder
course draining away. If she went to see Stacey or Samantha, she'd
refuse to eat there, insisting that she'd only eat my food at home.
She didn't want to be separated from me for a single moment.

I could see that this was a huge loss for Kaya. Much later, she
was able to explain it to me: 'When Lesley left, I felt that I'd lost
you both. Lesley walked out the door and you became so sad
and depressed, not the fun-loving, funny Mummy Jackie I knew.'

I had been the one encouraging her to climb trees, to throw snowballs and to take out her roller skates, saying, 'Don't worry. I'm here if you fall.' Lesley had been the sensible one, setting limits and bedtimes. Now, I became both Mam and Dad and my fears around losing Kaya too began to grow. I became anxious and watchful, constantly asking Kaya what she was doing. In fact, Kaya started doing counselling to deal with her feelings. I hadn't, yet, because I kept telling myself that I was doing okay. That the sadness and loneliness would pass.

One evening, Kaya returned from a visit to Lesley's. She bounced in and smiled at me, her little overnight bag on her lap. 'What's in there?' I asked her.

She reached into the bag and pulled out Mam's old smartphone. Mam loved taking photos so she'd upgraded to a new model and I'd passed her old one onto Lesley to use, asking her not to delete the photos, that I'd download them at some point.

My heart fluttered with anxiety. 'What are you doing with that?' I asked Kaya.

'I just wanted to look at Nana's photos,' she said. When I dug a little deeper, it turned out that Kaya had found the phone and taken it. 'I brought it home, because it's not hers; it's Nana's and I wanted to see photos of her and Grandad.' She looked at me with the innocence of a child and my heart sank. Kaya had taken something without asking permission and that was not good behaviour.

Kaya was grinning from ear to ear, delighted that she'd got precious memories back for her and for me. I looked at her sternly and held out my hand for the phone. *I'll deal with this later*, I thought, telling her to get ready for bed.

Much later that night, my curiosity got the better of me. I opened the phone and along with the photos were text messages from Lesley to friends and family. I shouldn't have looked but of course, I did. One message in particular stood out to me. YOU'RE FREE NOW. TEN YEARS LATER THAN PLANNED BUT FREE.

I ignored the rest of the message, the Christmas greetings, as the ground shifted from under me. I had been right in my sense that Lesley had been planning this all along. I began to think that the loving relationship I'd imagined had never really existed. *God*, I thought, *did she ever love me? Was I just a provider or did she ever love me for me?* All I'd wanted to do was to make Lesley happy and to be as good a person as I could possibly be so that she'd love me. I could make this work if I gave her everything. I knew that Lesley had been treated badly in the past, and I wanted to fix that, to show her what unconditional love could look like. In the process, I had given her myself, and when she'd left, the person I'd been left too.

Was that all our relationship had been, I began to wonder. *How had I got it so wrong?*

CHAPTER 22

LOSING IT ALL

Who is it that said you can never really know someone? I had spent 18 years with Lesley, the longest relationship of my life, apart from that with my family, and yet, I understood that I'd never know what was going on inside her head. As the weeks passed, I would find little things that pointed to another reality, one in which I had given my trust fully, even naively, only wanting love in return, and it was clear that Lesley saw things very differently. I felt totally at sea, nothing around me that was familiar, that I could fully put my faith in. As the 'daddy' of the family, I had provided, just like my own father did, for a shared future. Now, that future had been pulled out from under me and from Kaya. Everything I'd saved for, I'd paid for, was now gone.

At my lowest ebb, I spoke to a friend of mine. 'Listen, Jackie,' she said. 'You need help.' For the first time in my life, I agreed. Ironically, that help came through an organisation called Healing Hands, that had been set up to help people who had been in care. That wasn't why I was going, I told myself. I was going because of the broken relationship.

Before that, Kaya and I decided that we needed a break, so we went on holiday to the south of Spain. I've always loved the hot sunshine and Kaya loved splashing around in the pool and playing on the beach. We used to go every year, Lesley, myself and Kaya, to Lesley's parents' apartment, so maybe I should have chosen somewhere new. When I asked about the apartment, it was made clear to me that I was no longer part of the family, which was so hard for me to accept. I had always remained friends with my ex partners, from Tom to Fiona. Kaya's mam was still very much a part of our lives, visiting us often and keeping in touch with her daughter, even when her own life was too hard for her to manage. I had to accept that maybe other people didn't see things the way I did.

It was hard to go to a place that held such happy memories for us, but Kaya and I made new ones. We played in the sun and swam and relaxed and had fun together. A tiny part of the old Jackie came back, the fun-loving one, the one who loved to dance and to have fun. We'd send Mam back regular videos of us sitting in the shade of a parasol, cool drinks in front of us.

One morning, my sister called me. 'Now, there's no need to panic . . .' she began. At those words, who doesn't panic! Mam had had a stroke, but they'd caught it early, in the first hour. I began to pack a bag to come back, but later that afternoon, Mam called me. 'Don't come back, I'm fine.' I could see her in the video call, looking pale but otherwise her usual self. 'Enjoy your holiday,' she reassured me, as did my brother and sisters. Later that evening, Mam went home with my sister Caroline, who had moved into her house to look after her. Kaya and I flew home the following evening, eager to see Mam as quickly as possible.

Caroline rang me that day to say that she'd found Mam on the floor that morning. She'd had another stroke and now, she was no longer coherent. The video call that Kaya and I had made would be the last time we'd ever speak to her.

There was nothing the hospital could do now, except watch and wait. Mam was 77 but had suffered from ill health all her life. We weren't sure if she'd pull through.

It was now the August Bank Holiday of 2015. Dad had been gone three years and Lesley one. I'd gone away for the weekend, but drove back to Limerick on the Bank Holiday Monday and when Kaya and I got to the hospital, the nurses and doctors were rushing around as the machines attached to Mam beeped frantically. Could this be the end? A couple of days before that, we had all agreed to sign a Do Not Resuscitate order if she took another turn. Mam had made her wishes on this clear: her father had died after a stroke and she didn't want to have the same experience.

The staff managed to stabilise Mam and urged us to go home and have a break. We didn't even get to the roundabout down the road from the hospital when we got another call. 'You'd better come back,' the nurse said. We contacted the rest of the family, Caroline, Gerard, our nieces and nephews, Kaya and myself, we all gathered around her bed. Kaya held Mam's hand and rubbed it gently, seeming to sense that this would calm her, even though Kaya was only eight years old. I watched the pulse that beat slowly in her neck. We all spoke to her and told her that if she wanted to go to Dad, she wouldn't be alone. We were all there with her.

And then the pulse in her neck stopped. 'Caroline,' I said. 'Mam's gone.'

Caroline had been talking quietly to her daughters and she turned to me and said, 'Are you sure?'

I nodded. 'I've been watching the pulse getting slower and slower. She's gone.' I went out to find a nurse and said, 'Will you come in and check her?'

The nurse looked doubtful. 'We gave her something to help her sleep, so she's probably out for the count.' But she bustled down the corridor and went into the small hospital room. She checked Mam carefully before saying, 'You're right. She's gone.'

It's funny but my first thought was, *Now I'm an orphan.* I was 53 years of age and I was now an orphan. The one person who was fully mine was gone. It was a strange sensation. But I'd seen her pining for Dad over the past three years and the thought that she was with him now gave me a huge amount of comfort. I walked out of the hospital thinking, *she's where she wants to be. They're back together.*

I'm not superstitious, but after Mam's death, little things appeared in the cottage that told me she was near. A couple of small white feathers, the robin appearing once more; once, I saw two robins together. That was all the more remarkable, because robins are known to be territorial. It seemed that there were signs, all around me, that Mam and Dad were gone, but still somehow nearby. That Christmas, I was going to my daughter's for dinner with Kaya when I caught a glimpse of the little rose bush I'd planted when I'd moved in to Ardnacrusha. Every April and May it would bloom with beautiful yellow roses. Now, it was bare apart from one single, yellow rose.

Moments like these gave me so much comfort, to feel that Mam and Dad were still there in some way. And just like Dad's dressing gown, I came across Mam's slippers neatly tucked under the bench in the hall. After Dad died, she used to come out to my house and we put on a fire, got a bar of her favourite chocolate and watched a movie together. She'd arrive with her overnight bag, with her dressing gown, nightdress and slippers. 'She must have left them behind,' I said to myself, as I picked them up and put them beside the bed, so she'd be near me when I slept. Ten years later they're still there.

CHAPTER 23

FRIDAYS WITH JOHN

The first thing I told my counsellor, John, was that I felt so guilty for taking that weekend off. For not seeing Mam until it was too late. He looked at me and he said, 'Jackie, you needed that break. You've been through so much in the last three years and you gave yourself some time for you. You saw your need. Your mam would have wanted you to have that. Don't beat yourself up. Don't let two days of not being there spoil a whole lifetime.' He was right.

John soon became a huge part of my life. I was never the kind to make time for myself, but I started to make Friday mornings between nine and ten my time with John. He'd always start with the present asking me how I was and how my week had gone, innocent enough questions, and slowly but surely, I started to open up. With John, I went all the way back to my childhood to take a peek at little Jackie. What had started out as counselling to cope with the loss of Lesley, the deaths of Mam and Dad, became something much deeper. I began to look at myself at different stages of my life, the helpless young child in the Mount, the angry girl with the chip on her shoulder, the teenager looking for belonging and then my adult self, the one who wanted love more than anything else. I started to see all the ways that the

Mount had affected me: my lack of confidence, the problems I had with establishing boundaries, my habit of being a people-pleaser. John would often say to me, 'Look at little Jackie, what do you want to say to her?'

I would look in my mind's eye at her, at the helpless baby in her frilly white dress, and I would break down and cry and just repeat, 'I want to be loved, I want to be loved, I want to be loved, I want to be loved.' I knew how much I wanted Kaya and how much I loved her and I would think, *why didn't little Jackie get that? Why didn't she get that love? Why did life have to be so cruel?* I couldn't imagine Kaya in the Mount – it would break me – but I had gone there. Like Kaya, little Jackie needed protecting.

I also talked a lot to John about my identity. I remember telling him about going out one night to my local pub, Nancy Blakes. I love going there because the music is great. Now, I'm tall, and I've always worn my hair short. I was wearing jeans and a smart shirt when I popped into the Ladies. There were three girls inside, doing their make-up and one of them turned to me and said, 'Sorry, you're in the wrong toilet.' I was so upset, thinking, what would happen if a young androgynous girl walked in here and they'd said that to her? Instead of telling them straight, I made excuses for them, explaining that I was actually a woman, but had short hair and a deep voice. They apologised and of course, I instantly said, 'Oh, you're okay, it's my fault. My hair is short.'

With John I came to understand that I was apologising for my existence in so many ways. I had stayed with someone who didn't love me, I had stopped going out with my friends and even changed my appearance, all just to fit in and to be accepted.

This is how I saw myself, that I wasn't good enough; that the only way people would tolerate me was if I fitted into their world.

John asked me once why I always felt that I had to be the giver, not the receiver. 'What happens if you don't give?' he asked me.

'That's in my nature,' I protested. 'I like to make people feel welcome and at home.'

'Hang on,' he said. 'Let's say that you're at a party with a tray of sandwiches. What do you do with it?'

'I offer them around,' I said. 'I make sure that everyone has one.'

'What if there's nothing left for you?'

'It doesn't matter, as long as everyone else is happy.'

John let the silence hang. Then he said, 'What if you pop one of the sandwiches into your mouth and then go around with the tray?'

I had no idea what he meant.

'What if you look after your needs and then look after others?' The concept was completely alien to me. 'Look,' he explained, 'I'm not telling you not to be a giver: but do you ever give to the wrong people, or give too much and lose who you are in the process?'

This made sense to me. Then John dropped the bombshell: 'What if you put you first and make sure you're okay and then you can give to others what you can give?'

The simple example of the tray of sandwiches made complete sense to me, it was a huge realisation hitting home. If I ate my sandwich and then shared the rest around, the outcome would be the same for others and I wouldn't go hungry. It resonated with me literally as well, because of the role that food has played in my life. In the Mount we would often go hungry, so I got used to not putting my own hunger first, whether real or emotional. Food was either a punishment or a reward. As a result, I often wouldn't recognise that I was physically hungry. To this day I eat one meal a day on average. It's a good meal, but I still ration food as if I'm in the Mount. I'm getting better though: I've begun to eat the foods that I enjoy and that remind me of my childhood, like pig's tails, which may sound horrible, but they're very tasty and remind me of Mam and Dad.

John helped me to come to terms with the woman I had become and to begin to find the real Jackie, the one who lay behind the joker, the life and soul of the party, the one who was a grafter, a responsible parent, but who loved to dance and who loved romance too. I began to understand that in order to be myself, I didn't need to give everything I had: I could make space for myself and still be the Jackie who would help out in any way she could.

This all might sound simple but it took four years of hard work and reflection. At the end of the process, I was a strong woman, who had compassion for myself, and that made me a better mam, a better friend, a stronger woman. I reached out to my old teammates and even though we hadn't spoken in some time, they rallied round. My social life improved, but more to the point, I felt that I was surrounded by love and support.

And when Ellen came into my life, I was ready to trust in love again. This time it was different. When we met, I made a bold move, one that I would never have attempted in my old life – I declared my feelings straight out. I took a leap of faith, which was reciprocated, thankfully. Ultimately, in spite of the sparks that flew when we met, the relationship didn't work out because of complicated family situations, but I knew that I'd been fully myself and was accepted by Ellen as the real me. I'll always be grateful to her for seeing me as me.

I had to be on my own for the first time in a long time and that was good for me. I found out who I was when no-one was looking and it turned out that I liked myself. I also had the time to find out more about the other side of my family, the shadow side that I'd never had the courage to look into. Having done a DNA test in 2018, and found out that I wasn't just half-Jamaican after all: in fact, my DNA told me that I was 46% sub-Saharan African and 54% Irish. That 46% was a patchwork of Benin-Toga-Ivory Coast-Nigeria-Jamaica. That mirrored the direction of the slave trade from Africa through the Caribbean and onto America and Europe, which made complete sense to me. My father's ancestors would have been sent to sugar plantations on big estates in Jamaica and in the United States, which made me think of this part of myself in a very different way. But I know that in spite of this, I am still Jackie McCarthy O'Brien, daughter of Precious and Mickey O'Brien, who made me who I am.

As to my father, I never found him, but thanks to the wonder of DNA, I found a half-brother in Birmingham. A woman called Marianne got in touch to say that my profile matched that of her father, Michael. Marianne was also of mixed heritage and Michael's mam had been Irish too. *What are the chances,* I thought. Would I agree to meet them? I took another leap of faith and went to Birmingham to meet him. Michael was three inches shorter than me but we bore a striking resemblance to each other. We both have dyslexia, we both have similar mannerisms. My own son, Robert, resembles Michael in many ways. It was like looking into a mirror. I'm pleased to say that Michael has come to visit us all in Limerick and has become a welcome part of my patch-work family.

During my trip to Birmingham in 2021, I dropped in to see my auntie Marie. She was in a nursing home at this point, but still as lively as ever. What she told me about my father completely took me aback. 'Oh, I remember him well,' she said. 'He lived at the end of Addison Road and he came from a very well-to-do family.'

I was astonished. 'You knew where he lived? Why didn't you tell me?'

She sighed. 'Look, dating a Black man in 1961 was taboo. So when your mam became pregnant with you, she made up a story about being raped at a party so that people wouldn't judge her.'

At first, I didn't know what to make of this information. I had always thought that Mam had been the victim of rape, that I was the child of a rapist. When I told Michael this, he said, 'you must be so angry with your mother.'

'No, I'm not,' I admitted. 'I know that she told a lie, but I know why she told it.' Knowing how desperate Mam must have been and how hard she'd fought to keep me only made me love her all the more. She had never stopped loving me, even when I was taken away from her and to me, she was a hero. If I remained bitter about what had happened to me, the priests and nuns would have won and this was not going to happen. With this under-standing, I realised that I no longer needed to find my 'real' dad.

Mickey O'Brien was my dad. He had raised me with the values and the resilience I needed. He encouraged me to find myself in sport, to develop my talent and to have the self-discipline to see things through. And most of all, he was a man of deep principle, who made me who I am, who taught me everything I know.

Epilogue

So where am I now? As I write, I feel I've just come out the other side of a ten-year growth spurt. I found my voice in lockdown, following an article about me in *The 42*, an online sports magazine. The piece was about me being the first Black female to play both soccer and rugby, a record I'm proud to hold. Then I was asked to take part in a panel discussion on *The Claire Byrne Show* on RTÉ television, to mark the first anniversary of George Floyd's death. I have to admit, I was terrified. I travelled to Dublin with my daughter, Sam, not knowing what the hell I was doing there.

The panel was made up of people whom I was in awe of: Emer O'Neill, an activist, teacher and presenter, Conor Buckley, founder of sustainable clothing brand The Human Collective and son of activist Christine Buckley, as well as politicians, members of religious orders and law students. I felt so out of my depth.

We were introduced to Claire Byrne five minutes before the show started and I turned to her and said, 'I don't know what I'm doing here.'

She smiled at me and said, 'you'll be just fine.' Well, I was just fine. I spoke from my heart and said what was my truth. Claire gave me the closing statement and, in that moment, I became visible, not only to the audience, but to myself. After the show, RTÉ posted my closing statement on its social media and the phone hasn't stopped ringing since. I've been asked to tell my story all around the country, to children, to county councils, to industries, to people all over the world on webinars. The response was so positive.

Not long after the Claire Byrne show, I dropped into Sam's house and asked her what this thing called TikTok was and how I could use it. Over lockdown, Sam and her partner Christine had become very popular on the app, with a mixture of funny videos and dance routines. Jokingly, Sam said to me, 'You'll find a girlfriend on TikTok – it has a great LGBTQ+ following.' I was not in the market for a girlfriend, but before I left the house, I'd posted my first video. It was simple, telling people my age, where I lived and so on, but over the next year, the more videos I made, the more my confidence grew. I started to tell my life story and all the lessons I'd learned from it and it seemed to resonate with a lot of people. My videos take an honest look at the ups and downs of life: there's no fakery, it's just me in my dress code of pyjamas, Dad's old dressing gown, or when I'm feeling flash, a three-piece suit or even a tux. I get to be myself: dancing, singing, playing music, doing comedy – it's all there and it's all real.

After I posted the first few videos, people began to private-message me about how helpful my videos were: they wondered if I'd ever thought about writing a book. They thought that the story about how I kept getting up after every knock would inspire others. This gave me the courage to reach out to literary agent Marianne Gunn O'Connor. I was over the moon when she agreed to help me. Five publishers expressed an interest and when I spoke to them all, I decided to go with Eriu and Deirdre Nolan, because she understood where I wanted the book to go. I didn't want it to be a memoir of my time in an industrial school, or a sports book, or an LGBTQ+ book. It wasn't a book solely about my identity either, even though all of these things are part of my story.

Apart from having my children, one of my proudest moments has been being Grand Marshal of Limerick Pride. Limerick will always be my home and its people are my family. They have always got my back and understand me and allow me to be myself. One of my biggest challenges has been attending a gala to celebrate Black and Irish people. Tony Connolly's Menswear fitted me for a tux and I felt a million dollars. The only problem was, I was growing increasingly nervous the nearer it got to the event. At one point, I called Emer O'Neill, who was now a friend, to say that I wasn't sure if I could go. 'You have to go!' she said, inviting me to join her and her family. *Why am I so nervous*, I wondered. The answer came to me at two o'clock in the morning. All my life I've fought to prove that I'm Irish, that I belong in this country. I owed so much to Limerick and my country. I felt I was being disloyal to my Jamaican side. And I also felt a bit of a fake, because I didn't really know much about Jamaica, apart from my beloved Bob Marley

I got up the next morning and made a TikTok saying how I felt. That I had lived my 63 years trying to make people see past my colour and embrace me as Irish. Now, I said I could no longer just see myself as just being Irish. To make me feel whole, I had to be both. I didn't know how my followers would take it, but I needn't have worried. The response overall was, you're the most Irish person we know, but you're also Jamaican. Go and be proud of who you are. As I have never felt Black enough to be seen as Black and never White enough to be seen as White, where I sit can often feel like a lonely place. One comment in particular resonated with me: 'Maybe, Jackie, you're the one who brings us all together.'

I took a deep breath, put my tux on and off I went. I had been asked onto Beta Da Silva's music show on RTÉ 2FM before the ball and I was unbelievably nervous: the show was coming live from the ball, and he was going to talk to me about my sporting achievements. I confided in him that I felt a bit of an imposter at the ball and he said, 'I totally get where you're coming from, but you're a trailblazer and you're going to be celebrated because you've done us proud.'

I went into that room and for the first time in my life, I embraced who I am. That night, at the Black and Irish event, I embraced Jackie O'Halloran-O'Brien-McCarthy. For all that I am.

And as a welcome postscript to six months of reflection and hard graft, God blessed me once more. After learning to be by myself and to enjoy what I had: my four beautiful children, my wonderful friends, a kind, caring, beautiful woman came into my life to enhance the happiness I had worked so hard to find within myself. I wasn't looking for anyone when we began to chat on TikTok. But the more I got to know her, I knew I had no choice: despite all the hurt and pain relationships had brought me, I had to open my heart to her. When you find that kind of happiness at our age, you run with it.

Ismay is American, and I'm mad about her. She makes me smile, looking in her eyes and seeing the love that she has for me. When I hold her hand in mine, I feel ten feet tall. She calms my soul and soothes my heart. She has visited me here in the place that will always be my home and has fitted in perfectly.

We talked constantly for almost a year, I had asked every question I could think of and I had seen no red flags.

Without planning it, last March, I took her to a jeweller's shop in Limerick, and after telling her the significance of the Claddagh ring, I selected one and placed it on her finger, pointing to her heart. The Claddagh ring has everything for me – loyalty in the crown, friendship in the hands and love in the heart. I looked into her eyes and hoped she'd understand what my heart was asking. 'Will you start the next chapter with me?' I didn't need to hear her answer – her eyes told me yes.

If ever anything was meant to be in my life, this is it. I feel my mother's presence everywhere, I see white feathers all the time, so much so we got them tattooed on our arms. I'm even moving back to Kileely. Ismay and I have bought a little house on the same road I grew up on. I can see Thomond Park from my bedroom window again, just as I did when I was a child. I'm going home to Kileely, bringing the love of my life with me and Little Jackie is in there too. This house will be our home.

So, there you have it. If I can leave you with one thing after reading this book, it is that no matter how bad life can get, it's always up to you to keep believing in yourself, to keep getting up, to never give up on your dreams, to work hard – 'It won't be handed to you,' as Dad would say. As I start a new chapter of life with my partner beside me, I am grateful to God, to my mam and my dad, to my family and my friends – to everyone who gave me the strength to get through the darkness. To see that the future can be bright, if I just let my light shine through.

ACKNOWLEDGEMENTS

I have so many people to thank for helping me to get this book down on paper. Marianne Gunn O'Connor for taking my call and believing that I had a story to tell. Deirdre Nolan from Bonnier Books, for understanding that this was a life story and not a sports book and for allowing me to tell my story, my way. To Alison Walsh, for the hours of listening to me and for helping to guide me on the order my story should take. To the people of Limerick for always having my back and giving me a home. To the wonderful friends I met on TikTok who watched me tell my life story and encouraged me to put it down on paper.

To my sports family of Green Park, Old Crescent, Shannon, Munster and Ireland, you saved my life, both on and off the pitch. To Rita Spring and to my wonderful friends, who showed me unconditional love when I most needed it. I can never thank you enough for the support you have given me over the years. To my amazing family, the O'Hallorans and the O'Briens, my sisters Caroline and Gina, my brothers Gerard and Michael. To my heartbeat, my children Sam, Robert, Stacey and Kaya; to my grandchildren, Aaliyah, Mason, Jaden – Nana loves you all so very much.

To the wonderful woman who makes my heart leap when she holds my hand, calms my soul and soothes my heart. I'm so excited to take the next step with you in life, Ismay. To my heroes, my mam and dad, Precious and Mickey O'Brien: I carry you in my heart each day, can feel your presence guiding me and loving me still. I hope that I have made you as proud of me as I am of you, always.

THE LIFE OF LEO XIII

Leo V. J. XIII.

THE LIFE OF LEO XIII

FROM AN AUTHENTIC MEMOIR
FURNISHED BY HIS ORDER

*Written with the Encouragement, Approbation
and Blessing of
His-holiness the Pope*

by

Bernard O Reilly, D.d., L.d.,
(Laval.)

MEDIATRIX PRESS
MMXVII

ISBN: 978-1-953746-12-2

Mediatrix Press
607 E. 6th Ave.
Post Falls, ID 83854
www.mediatrixpress.com